magritte

magritte

Text by
PAMELA PRITZKER

LEON AMIEL • PUBLISHER
NEW YORK

Published by
LEON AMIEL • PUBLISHER
NEW YORK
ISBN 0-8148-0627-9
Printed in the United States of America

INTRODUCTION

Seldom in the history of Twentieth Century Art has there been an artist as profoundly enigmatic as Rene Magritte. He was a painter of poetry and revelation, for whom the essence of painting, ". . . consists in representing through pictorial technique the *unforeseen* images that might appear to me, whether my eyes are open or shut."

Unlike other Surrealist artists, Magritte did not utilize the realm of sleeping dreams. Rather, he drew upon the images of the waking world. He depicted simple representations of objects, misplaced and rearranged by his desire to transcend the apparent mediocrity of the every day world. Magritte chose to present us with the true mystery and poetry within our existence.

BIOGRAPHY

Magritte referred to very few childhood memories, in fact he stated, "I detest my past and anyone else's." The few events that he chose to reveal were always imbued with a sense of mystery and often reappear as visual themes in his later works.

Rene Magritte was born on November 21, 1898, in Lessines, Belgium, located midway between Charleroi and the North Sea. Very early in life, he experienced a vision-like image of a large wooden chest quite close to his crib. This image of a heavy, wooden textured object reappears throughout Magritte's painting. At the age of one, his family moved to Gilly, a smaller and less cosmopolitan town. Shortly after the move, two balloonists arrived at his home. Their costumes of leather pants, jackets, goggles and helmets seemed to young Magritte quite macabre. They proceeded to drag from the roof of Magritte's house their balloon which had become entangled on the pitch. This occurrence would remain engraved in his imagination for many years to come. Shortly thereafter, Magritte and his family moved to Chatelet where, at the age of twelve, he began to draw and paint. On Sundays, he would study pyrogravure and painting in a makeshift classroom in a local store.

During his youth, many vacations were spent in the company of his grandmother and aunts in Soignies. To pass the summer months, he and a neighbor would play in a nearby cemetery among the granite markers and tombs. Together, they would frequently explore the underground vaults. On one occasion, as they ascended from the dark vault into daylight, he sighted an artist from the city painting the scenery. The artist was seated amidst the dead autumn leaves and crumbled ruins of ancient tombstones. This event was full of wonder and mystery for Magritte. Much later in life, Magritte, recalling it, stated, "[The artist] . . . seemed to me to be performing magic! When I began to paint myself, toward 1915, the memory of that enchanted encounter with painting oriented my efforts in a direction having little to do with common sense."

Another pastime which never ceased to intrigue Magritte was dressing up as a priest. He would stand in front of a homemade altar and perform a mock mass in the utmost seriousness. At other times, he would rush about in a religious frenzy frightening his entire family. Whether these episodes betokened an earnest, religious zeal or were simply an escapade in the absurd, we shall never know. However, Magritte continued to be fascinated with the mysteries shrouding all religious ceremonies and their accompanying sacred paraphenalia.

In 1912, a tragic event struck the Magritte

household. In the middle of the night, Magritte's youngest brother Paul awoke to discover their mother was missing. He aroused the rest of the family and the search began. They discovered her drowned in the River Sambre, with her nightgown covering her head. The cause of death remained unknown. Magritte had childhood memories of the odd manner in which people began to act towards him. As the son of the 'dead woman' he took pride in the attention that he suddenly received. As we shall see further on, the image of a covered face reoccurs in the later works of Magritte.

After his wife's death, Magritte's father moved the family to Charleroi and engaged nurses and a governess to oversee his very active sons. Following grade school, Magritte studied the classics at the Athenee in Charleroi where he had a chance encounter with Georgette, his future wife. In 1916, he left the Athenee out of boredom with academia and enrolled in the Academy of Beaux-Arts in Brussels. Two years later, the entire Magritte family joined him in Brussels. Magritte at this time began to develop his career as an artist and founded many friendships which would last his entire life.

The following year Magritte, together with the poets Pierre Bourgeois and Pierre Flouquet, published a contemporary review, entitled: *Au Volant*! 1919 also marked the year of his first exhibited painting, "Three Women," at the Galerie Giroux. This painting clearly showed the influence of Picasso and Cubism. In 1920, he met E.L.T. Mesens, the Belgian Surrealist poet, musician and collagist. Together they wrote Surrealist poems and prose. The prose of Magritte is not generally known. He did write a detective story, but it was never published. His interest in the invincible detective is further evident in his immense enjoyment of the French mystery series, *Fantomas*, the American stories by Dashiel Hammett and Rex Stout, and the weekly tales of Nick Carter and Nat Pinkerton. Magritte was also an avid fan of the cinema. While still a child, he and his brothers would spend afternoons devouring the various American silent thrillers such as *The Perils of Pauline*.

In 1920, Magritte, while walking down the streets of Brussels on his way to an appointment, ran into Georgette. When she inquired where he was going, he replied that he was on his way to visit his mistress. Despite this inauspicious beginning, they were married two years later and remained so until Magritte's death in 1967.

In order to support his family, Magritte worked as a commercial artist, painting wallpaper designs and creating advertising layouts. His own creative work was restricted to his free evenings. His style at this time was uncertain, but he felt greatly inspired by a Futurist illustrated catalogue a friend had sent to him. However, nothing would seduce Magritte into pursuing traditional aesthetic goals. As he so pointedly stated, "... undoubtedly one pure and powerful sentiment, eroticism, kept me at that time from falling into a more traditional search for formal perfection. The only thing I wanted to provoke was an emotional shock." This desire to shock, which is omnipresent in his works, made Magritte a unique and individual man.

1922-1925

The next three years witnessed Magritte's emergence as an artist. Magritte's painting, "Portrait of Pascal" (since destroyed), revealed a similarity to the works of De Chirico. Yet, Magritte was unacquainted with those works until some months later, when Marcel Lecomte showed him a copy of De Chirico's, "The Song of Love." It had an instantaneous and overwhelming impact on Magritte. In a letter written in 1965 to James Thrall Soby, Magritte recalled the event. "It was in fact in 1922 when I first came to know the works of Chirico. A friend showed me a reproduction of his painting, 'The Song of Love,' which I always consider to be a work by the greatest painter of our time in the sense that it deals with poetry's ascendancy over painting and the various manners of painting. Chirico was the first to dream of WHAT MUST BE PAINTED and not HOW TO PAINT."

De Chirico's work had a similar impact upon the Parisian Surrealists, including Breton and Yves Tanguy. However, none incorporated his principles as closely in their work as did

Magritte in his constant search to represent "poetry's ascendancy over painting."

In 1925, he and E.L.T. Mesens founded *Oesophage*, a single issue review whose motto, "Hop la!, Hop li!" was very much in keeping with the work and spirit of Francis Picabia. This issue was soon followed by three issues of *Marie*, ". . . a bimonthly paper for the beautiful young people." Within months, Mesens and Magritte joined ranks with Marcel Lecomte, Andre Souris, Paul Nouge and Camille Goemans (who later opened the first Surrealist gallery in Paris) to form the core of the Belgian Surrealist group.

Mesens acted as a liaison between the Belgian and Parisian Surrealists. He was in constant contact with Breton and Marcel Duchamp. They sent him their latest pamphlets, reviews and kept him informed of the latest scandalous Surrealist activities. Yet, Magritte remained aloof from the stringent theories and dogma the faithful Surrealists followed.

That same year, Magritte painted or as he stated, "first realized painting," in "The Lost Jockey." Although the original was lost, he repainted the image in 1940. He introduced into his own works the 'poetic idea' and left behind all formal investigations. He was to follow this practice the rest of his career. As the first work to come after the discovery that painting could go beyond its traditional function, "The Lost Jockey" represents a new reality: a poetic reality. We are confronted by a jockey riding a horse through a forest of balusters *(bilboquets)* from which sprout branches and leaves. To the far right corner there appears a full length curtain. It is impossible to explain this painting in terms of a rational or causal solution. This inability to apply a logical explanation to his paintings, became a primary criterion of success to Magritte. We cannot rearrange the images into a rational and comforting picture. We must rearrange the 'furniture' of our minds to comprehend his paintings. It is the mystery of the work which denies us a causal explanation and forces us to stretch and expand beyond what we had heretofore known as the 'real.'

The motif of the balusters is one of Magritte's iconographic trademarks. In each new painting the identity of the object shifts, as does its power to evoke new fears of the unknown. In "The Difficult Crossing," which he first painted in 1926, the *bilboquet* becomes a spectator standing and 'observing' a storm tossed ship. In the 1963 version, the *bilboquet* has one cyclopic eye and is garbed in a suit. 'He' is standing with 'his' back to the stormy sea in front of a statue-like *bilboquet*. Thus, he reworked the theme into many different and evocative identities. As we shall see, Magritte's career is marked by his constant attempts to solve the same visual and philosophical problems which first appear during this period in the late 1920s. "The Lost Jockey" is a perfect example of his attempts to solve one particular problem. It was first painted in 1925, then in 1926, 1940, 1942 and in 1960 we find variations on the theme in "The Childhood of Icarus" and "The Wrath of the Gods." Finally, in 1965, the jockey himself is transformed into a woman riding a horse in "Carte Blanche." Therefore, at times a standard chronological history of Magritte's work is useless. It is far more relevant to trace the visual development of his numerous ideas and concepts.

During 1926, Magritte viewed for the first time two of Paul Eluard's Surrealist poetry books. Both *Repetitions* and *Les Malheurs Des Immortels* were illustrated with outstanding collages by the German Surrealist, Max Ernst. The effect of Ernst's collages on Magritte was similar in its force to that of De Chirico's works. Magritte wrote, "In illustrating *Repetitions*, by Paul Eluard, Max Ernst has demonstrated magnificently that through collages obtained from old magazine illustrations, one could easily surpass everything which gives traditional painting its prestige . . ." Magritte had found two kindred spirits in his search to go beyond the traditional boundaries of painting.

In the two year period of 1925-1927, Magritte furiously painted his newly discovered ideas into images, at the rate of one painting per day. All of the motifs, elements and images which were to appear in his later works made their debut. In 1927, at the Galerie Le Centaute in Brussels, he had his first one man show. Included in the exhibition was "The Lost Jockey," "The Difficult

Crossing," "The Threatened Assassin," "Dawn At Cayenne" and twelve assorted collages. Although the show was not particularly successful, P.G. Van Hecke, the owner of the gallery, became Magritte's patron. His generosity afforded Magritte the opportunity to leave his job as a commercial artist and become a full time painter.

Shortly after the exhibition, Magritte left Brussels for a three year sojourn in France. For several months he lived in Paris, then in August, 1927, he settled in Perreaux-sur-Marne, a suburb of Lyons. Although he remained in contact with Breton and Eluard, he avoided all political affiliations with the Parisian group. He stayed out of their debates on the morality of the Communist Party and other socialist movements. He remained uninvolved and distant, a position which he sustained throughout most of his life.

Magritte's work during his three years in France tended to be of sombre colors, highly dramatic and always mysterious. The spatial settings are misleading; the characters are bizarre and lurking. The atmosphere of the works tends to reflect Magritte's interest in contemporary culture. The late 1920's were characterized by the riotous Charleston, the dramatic eroticism of the tango, the films of Chaplin and Valentino and the fabulous adventure stories of *Fantomas*. In fact, Fantomas became the hero-at-large for the French Surrealists. He was the invincible perpetrator of the most evil and heinous crimes. Yet in all thirty volumes of his exploits, Fantomas, not the detective, is the undeniable hero. Imagine how Magritte felt about a creature who defied logic and reason by outraging society, outwitting the police and still remained the hero! When the thriller was finally made into a film, the popularity of Fantomas soared. The film version became a favorite of Appolinaire, who was the leading Surrealist writer and poet. Visually, Fantomas was even more daring and treacherous. He stalked the streets of Paris in a myriad of disguises, always covering his face. His true identity remained a mystery.

Magritte was enthralled by the escapades of Fantomas. In 1943, he painted "The Backfire," which was based on a Fantomas book cover. In

1928, he captured the quintessence of the Fantomas character in his painting, "The Savage." It is a portrait of a man in a top hat and eye-mask. He is leaning his chin on the palm of his hand. Sections of his face and shoulders fade out to reveal the brick wall in the background. This is Fantomas: visible one moment, then gone; everywhere, yet nowhere. Magritte discovered in Fantomas the essential dialectic of life: 'being and nothingness'.

It was during this period that Magritte painted "The Threatened Assassin." It is quite impossible to view this painting and not think of a Fantomas-like crime. A young, nude woman lies dead on a sofa. Her presumed murderer, a well-dressed young man, is in the same room listening to the gramaphone. His hat and coat are thrown over a chair, and a valise is on the floor. Two men stand outside the entrance to the room. One holds a limb-shaped club; the other readies a net. They appear to be about to capture the killer. As our eye moves further back into the space we see three male faces peering over the window into the room, perhaps there to prevent the killer from escaping. Even further back we see the erotic slopings of a mountain range. The spatial dimensions are extremely deep. Magritte moves us from outside the room, to inside the room, to outside again through the window. Yet, there is still another exterior point of view, our own as spectator. Magritte had begun to explore the philosophical problem of looking from the outside into the world. We view the world not from within, but as spectators or members of an audience, a problem which he attempted to deal with in many of his works.

Another disturbing aspect of "Assassin" is the manner in which it depicts human beings. They have very little facial expression, as if they were wearing masks. They function as objects do in 'real' life. There is no mistaking the figures for living human beings. Magritte has presented us with another dialectical problem. Represenations of men could also be representations of manikins, or copies of copies of copies of copies. It is as if the figures were inanimate chess pieces waiting to be moved by a giant looming hand.

He has painted a human still-life and, by doing so, reinforced the basic fictional character of all painting.

Two other paintings from this same period evoke a similar mysterious and frightening sensation. In "The Lovers," we see a man and a woman from the shoulders up, with their heads covered by a flowing cloth. In "The Heart of the Matter," a woman is standing behind a table on top of which is a tuba and a valise. She supports her neck with one, and her head is also covered by a bag-like cloth. One possible source for these two macabre images is the film of Fantomas, whose face and, at times, head were covered. A second and perhaps hidden source was the manner in which Magritte's mother was discovered: drowned, with her nightgown thrown over her head.

Earlier, we spoke of Magritte's youthful interest in the cinema. During the years 1928-1930, he began dividing his canvas into frames, much like the celluloid frames of film. He applied this technique in "The Six Elements," "On The Threshold of Liberty" and "Man

Reading A Newspaper." The first consists of six asymmetrical, flattened wooden frames containing six seemingly unrelated images. They include fire, a woman's torso, a forest, an exterior of a house, clouds and heavy harness bells. The following year, Magritte dramatized this concept into the stage-like three-dimensional "On The Threshold of Liberty." In addition, he added a cannon pointed at the woman's torso and a wall of cut-outs. Magritte's work reorganizes elements from our everyday world into opposing and contrasting rhythms. It rings out with poetic imagery which jars our mental set of preconceptions. The third framed painting, "Man Reading A Newspaper" is just as the title describes. However, after the first frame, the man and his newspaper both disappear. We are left with the trite setting of a bourgeois living room. The absence of man from his environment makes absolutely no difference; everything remains the same.

An imposing influence on Magritte and the Surrealists was the Nineteenth Century prosepoem "Les Chants De Maldoror." It was written by the Comte de Lautreamont, nom de plume of Isadore Ducasse, who died at the age of twenty-four. The images in "Maldoror" derive their fundamental absurdity from a lack of any rational relationship. This is best explained by Lautreamont's now famous statement: "As beautiful as . . . the fortuitous encounter on an operating table of a sewing machine and an umbrella." This brief phrase became the modus operandi for many Surrealist artists.

Maldoror was very similar to Fantomas, especially in his ability to change identities at will. He was an Einsteinian superman who could be all over the world at any one time. He was also the arch-enemy of the police and society. They could not capture Maldoror, for like Fantomas, he was substance, then spirit, flesh then ashes. In 1938, Magritte contributed one drawing to a new edition of "Les Chants De Maldoror." Ten years later he illustrated a complete edition of "Maldoror," with seventy-seven drawings.

After three years in France, Magritte had become disgusted with the doctrinal attitudes of the Surrealists. He could not abide by their experimental techniques and methods, nor with their obsessive desire to express only dream images. Following one last argument, he and Georgette returned to Brussels. There Magritte found a new and enlarged circle of Belgian Surrealist artists, sculptors and poets.

ILLUSION AND REALITY

The 1930s marked the period of Magritte's highest virtuosity as an artist, explorer and philosopher. He concretized the various ideas and problems which had been hinted at in the earlier works and brought them to complete visual fruition.

Ever since the Renaissance, painting had been the presentation of a three-dimensional reality on a two-dimensional surface. This led to numerous techniques of perspective drawing and painting. However, the use of perspective is nothing more than a method of tricking the eye into seeing three-dimensional space on the flat surface of the canvas. This contradiction between reality and illusion was defined in Magritte's "The Human Condition I" (1933). In this painting we are confronted by the ultimate dialectic of seeing 'reality' in a work of art. In describing "The Human Condition I," Magritte stated, "The problem of the window led to 'La Condition Humaine.' In front of a window, as seen from the interior of a room, I placed a picture that represented precisely the portion of landscape blotted out by the picture. For instance, the tree represented in the picture displaced the tree situated behind it, outside the room. For the spectator it was simultaneously inside the room, in the picture, and outside, in the real landscape, in thought. Which is how we see the world, namely outside of us, though having only one representation of it within us."

Thus, Magritte visually explored the tension between reality and illusion. He showed the impossibility of reconciling the inherent differences between the real space we live in and the illusionist space of the canvas. This reversal of Renaissance aesthetics is probably the one essential element of Twentieth Century Art.

In "The Human Condition II" (1935), Magritte utilized the same basic concept but altered the landscape to a seascape. Again, we are confronted by a multi-illusion. We observe an easel with a canvas placed in front of an arched window behind which is the sea. The very portion of the seascape which is blocked by the canvas is depicted on the canvas. Yet, it is impossible to distinguish which is in fact 'real' sea and which is the represented portion. Moreover, we must not forget that the entire image is a representation. Once again, Magritte displayed the conflict of illusion and reality. We are presented with ambiguities of action and identity within the interior world of thought and the exterior world of action. According to Magritte, the way in which we see the world is, ". . . as being outside ourselves even though it is only a mental representation of it that we experience inside ourselves."

Magritte used the window as the twilight zone through which we pass from inside to outside. He applied this image in a variety of ways. In "Evening Falls," we see a shattered window through which we view a landscape and a setting sun. The same image appears on the fragments of shattered glass. A similar device is found in "The Domain of Arnheim," the title of which was taken from Edgar Allan Poe's story. Again, we see a shattered window pane with segments of the outside mountain scape on them.

In numerous works, which span well into the 1960s, Magritte continued to use the images of the window and the easel in his attempt to solve the dichotomy of reality and illusion. In the 1930s he added to his repertoire of problems, the image of the door. Like the window, the door affords us passage from the inside to the outside. In "The Unexpected Answer" and "Amorous Perspective," Magritte has placed huge gaps in the doors. The gaps appear to be the result of someone literally charging through the wooden doors to get to the outside. In the first work, the other side of the door is a vast fading darkness, which becomes pitch blackness as we try to see further back into space. In "Amorous Perspective," we see a huge tree leaf placed to the side of a two-story house. We never know what the door will open to us, or if anything at all will be there. But we do want to know exactly what is hidden from our eyes.

While Magritte was developing his inside/outside theme, he began to explore the essential differences between the object and that which represents the object. In "The Waterfall," we see an easel on which is a painting of a forest. These are placed within the lush green leaves of the painted forest. Magritte has given us a painting-within-a-painting. But the painting of the forest is no longer outside the actual forest, but within it. Magritte has taken two different spatial orders which are so intrinsically linked together that their respective locations suddenly become possible through thought. As he stated, ". . . It is only thought which can see itself simultaneously in the forest and away from the forest."

In all of these paintings Magritte examined the differences, be they subtle or obvious, between the real object and its representation. He tried to force the observer to understand this idea and to be able to see that a painted representation is only an illusion of reality. As is often found in his work, it is the image of an intangible idea or thought.

WORDS AND IMAGES

Magritte did not use painting as an end in itself. He used it to provoke a certain shock to the sensibilities, as a contradiction to our past knowledge of reality. During his search into the conflict of illusion and reality, Magritte also discovered that the name given to an object, as with its representation, is not the object, nor does it have much in common with the object. He knew that words are meant as symbols for objects, yet one object may be referred to in a variety of ways. Magritte began to paint a series of works which were in part words. In "The Use of Words I," (1928-1929), we see a pipe under which is found the words, "Ceci n'est pas une pipe" (this is not a pipe). In fact it is not a pipe, but a painting of the object we call a 'pipe.' He continued to paint versions of the pipe, each time expressing a deeper paradox between the spoken, written and painted word and the object. In "The Air and the Song" (1964) and "The Two Mysteries" (1966) by repeating the motif, Magritte demonstrated the inadequacies of language and all symbols. As he summed up, "Whatever the strokes, the words, and the colors arranged on a page, the figure obtained is always full of meaning."

Magritte soon discovered the random relationship between the object and its name. As many writers have since pointed out, Magritte's explorations into the 'relative' nature of names were very similar to writings of the now famous Wittgenstein. He moved closer and closer towards his goal of breaking down the traditional concept of a word always being equivalent to a specific object. As he stated, "Sometimes the name of an object replaces an image. A word can replace an object in real life. An image can replace a word in a proposition."

This is ever so clear in "The Magical Mirror" (1928-1929) in which we find written across the surface of a hand mirror, "corps humain."

Magritte grasped the interchangeability between an object and its name. With this understanding, he moved further away from the pursuits of the Surrealists. He began to change the function of painting from one of static depiction, to one of questioning the fundamental basis of all communication.

In "The Key of Dreams" (1930) Magritte painted six objects within their own frames. Under each object is a totally unrelated name. He reworked the traditional object/name relationship which he explained in "Words and Images": "An object is not so stuck on its name that one can't find another." Before modern linguistics became a recognized science, Magritte came to understand the arbitrary nature of words and the things they represent.

HEGEL'S UMBRELLA

Much Surrealist art is devoted to the juxtaposition of unrelated objects. It was felt that a new beauty, much like Lautreamont's umbrella and sewing machine, could evolve out of chance relationships between dissimilar objects. Magritte did not follow this line of exploration. He chose to seek the hidden similarities between objects (e.g.) mouth to glass, glove to hand. He developed a complex methodology and tightly controlled all elements of visual shock. His method did not rest upon chance or automatism. Each potential combination had been worked and reworked in small drawings until he finally came upon the correct combination of objects. A.M. Hammacher aptly described this search as an attempt to "achieve a controlled resonance."

Although Magritte had been delving into this concept in much of his earlier work, it was not until 1936 that he became fully aware of his own method. In his writings, Magritte recalled the incident which suddenly changed his pursuits: "One night in 1936, I awoke in a room in which a cage and the bird sleeping in it had been placed. A magnificent error caused me to see an egg in the cage instead of the bird. I then grasped a new and astonishing poetic secret, because the shock I experienced had been provoked precisely by the affinity of two objects, the cage and the egg, whereas I used to provoke this shock by causing the encounter of unrelated objects."

Magritte turned this revelation into an avid pursuit for new, but related, combinations of objects. This included combining a bicycle and a cigar in "State of Grace" (1959) and a cigar with a fish in "Homage to Alphonse Allais" (1964). Yet, Magritte reminds us it is not a cigar we see nor a real fish; it is the 'painting' we see of both.

On the basis of this principle, Magritte began to deal with the problem of depicting the images of women, rain, cellos, carrots and clouds. In "Hegel's Holiday," Magritte chose the images of a glass of water resting atop an open umbrella. The images also have fluctuating identities. They never remain static or immobile. He created a single painting containing an infinite amount of possibilities. He constantly painted multi-valent images whose meaning is never absolute. In "The Battle of Argonne" (1959) Magritte took two known objects, a cloud and a boulder, and floated them both in a moonlit sky. By placing these together as weightless objects,

Magritte contradicted our previous knowledge about the weight of the boulder. He also positioned them in a peculiar manner to confuse their actual location. Do they float upwards, downwards or are they suspended above the earth? These are the possibilities which Magritte has forced us to confront. As in all of his work, the questions one asks are perhaps more important than knowing the answers.

LATE 1940s AND 1950s

Following World War II, Magritte's preoccupation with death dominated his work. In "Perspective: The Balcony By Manet" (1949) Magritte took Manet's charming nineteenth century painting of a balcony filled with his friends and replaced the friends with coffins. However, the coffins have been imbued with human poise, and in a perverse sense they invite us to join them. The second of this 'coffin' series, "Perspective: Madame Recamier By David," refers to an earlier David painting of Madame Recamier reclining on a chaise. Here also

Magritte replaced the human figure with a 'reclining' coffin. One is reminded of David's "Marat" as well, in which Marat lies dying in his bathtub. The posing of the coffin as a human being shocks the spectator, yet at the same time makes one extremely sensitive to the magic in life.

During the 1950s, Magritte became fascinated with all forms and sizes of rocks. In addition to being entranced by their textures, he attached great importance to their monumentality and power to subdue all nature. Magritte's work in his 'Stone Age' period ranged from the giant floating boulder in "The Castle in the Pyrenees" to the ossified apple and pear in the "Recollection of Travels" series.

At the same time, Magritte continued his explorations into the illusion of reality. In one of his most famous works, "Personal Values," Magritte has taken personal objects and placed them in a bedroom. However in addition to changing the proportions of the objects he replaced the bedroom walls with a cloudy, tranquil sky. Magritte enlarged the comb to be twice the size of the double bed; the wine glass is as large as the mirrored armoire, etc. By changing the sizes of the various objects, Magritte has irreparably altered their relationships. Yet, "Personal Values" does not seem unbelievable. Within the context Magritte has created, just as in Lewis Carroll's *Alice In Wonderland*, everything is possible and all things are relative.

In June, 1967, Magritte began a new project which unfortunately he was not to complete. He embarked on a journey into the 'real' three-dimensionality of sculpture. He planned to construct eight pieces based upon themes found in the following paintings: "Madame Recamier by David," previously mentioned, "The White Race," "The Well of Truth," "The Natural Graces," "The Golconda," "The Labors of Alexander," "Delusions Of Grandeur" and "The Therapeutist." Although five copies of each cast were eventually exhibited, he did not live to see the first casting. On August 15, 1967, Magritte died in Brussels, never to complete this last exploration.

LIST OF PLATES

38 Hegel's holiday 1958
Private collection, Brussels

39 The large family 1947
Private collection, Knokke le Zoute

40 The victory 1939
Private collection, Paris

41 The enchanted domain 1952
Salle du Lustre, Casino de Knokke le Zoute

42 Untitled

43 The beautiful captive

44 The key to the fields 1933
Claude Spaak Collection, Paris

45 At the threshold of liberty
Museum Boymans Van Beuningen, Rotterdam

46 The break of day 1967
Private collection

47 Perpetual motion 1934
Eric Estorick Collection, London

48 The enchanted domain 1950
Salbe du Lustre, Knokke le Zoute

49 Passionflower 1936

50 The voice of the winds 1932
Peggy Guggenheim Foundation, Venice

51 The rose model 1947
Private collection, New York

52 Philosophy in the bedroom 1947
Thomas Claburn Jones Collection, New York

53 The dress of night 1954
Private collection

54 The rape 1934
Private collection, London

55 The enchanted domain 1952
Salle du Lustre, Casino de Knokke le Zoute

56 Summer walks 1938
Claude Spaak Collection, Paris

57 The enchanted domain (detail) 1952
Salle du Lustre, Casino de Knokke le Zoute

58 Madame Recamicr by David 1950
Private collection, Brussels

59 Manet's balcony 1950
Musee des Beaux Arts, Gand

60 The schoolmaster 1954
Private collection, Paris

61 Order's friend 1964
Private collection, Chicago

62 The month of the harvest 1959
Private collection

63 The ready-made bouquet (detail) 1956
Private collection

64 Title Unknown

65 The flavor of tears 1948
Musee Royaux des Beaux Arts, Brussels

66 The enchanted domain (detail) 1952
Salle du Lustre, Casino de Knokke le Zoute

67 The enchanted domain (detail) 1952
Salle du Lustre, Casino de Knokke le Zoute

68 Arnheim's domain 1962
Private collection, Brussels

69 The rights of man, 1947
Private collection, Milan

70 Untitled

71 The thief 1967
Private collection

72 When the time is up (detail) 1946
Private collection

73 The meeting with pleasure, 1950
Private collection, New York

74 Memory 1948
Collection Administration des Beaux Arts, Brussels

75 Memories of a saint 1961
Private collection, Houston

76 Spring (detail) 1965
Private collection

77 Man with the melon hat 1964
Private collection, New York

78 The difficult crossing, 1963
Alexandre Iolos Collection, Paris

79 Reveries of a solitary walker (detail) 1926
Private collection, Brussels

PLATES

1
The Golconde (detail)
1953

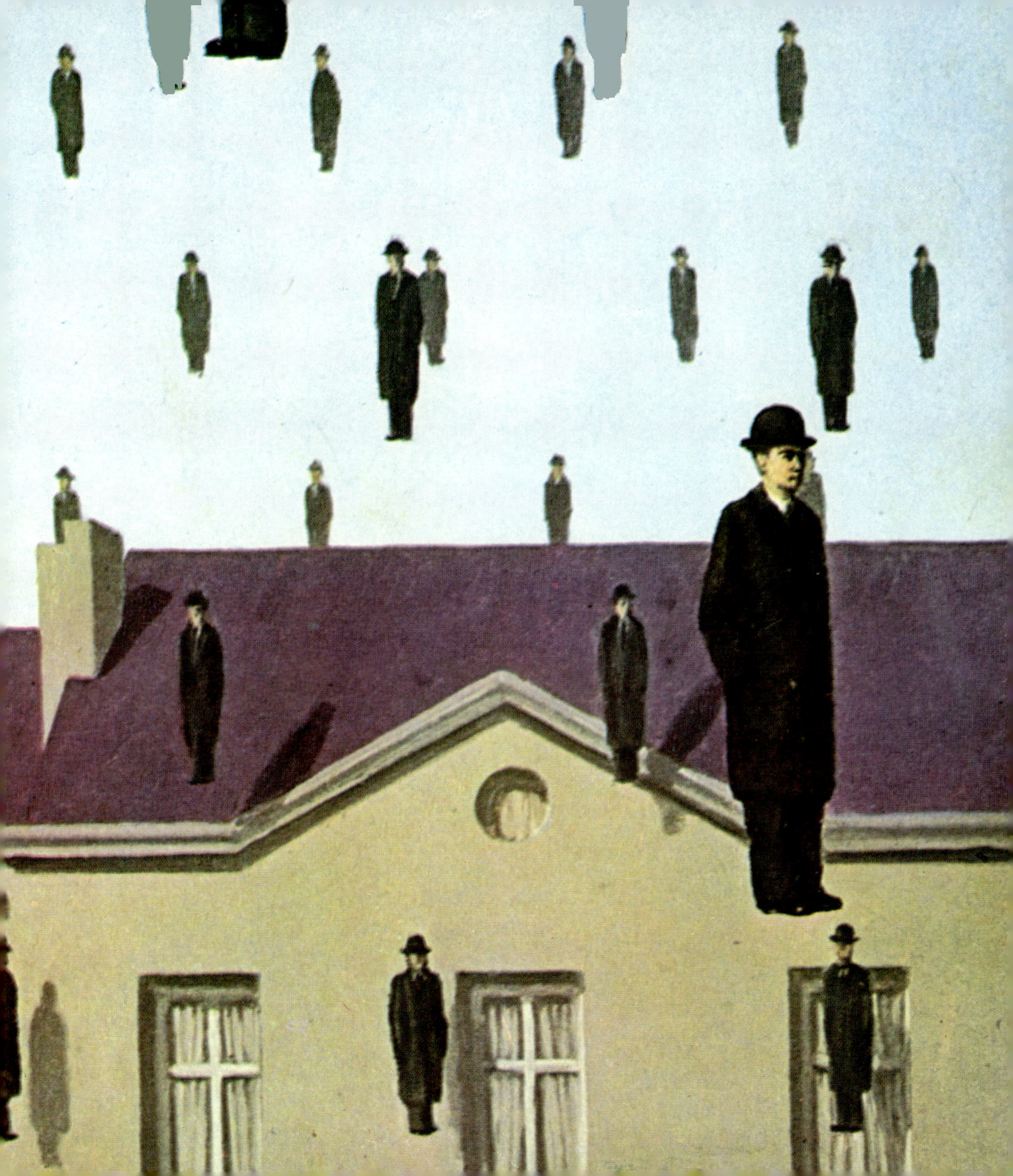

2
The threatened assassin (detail)
1926

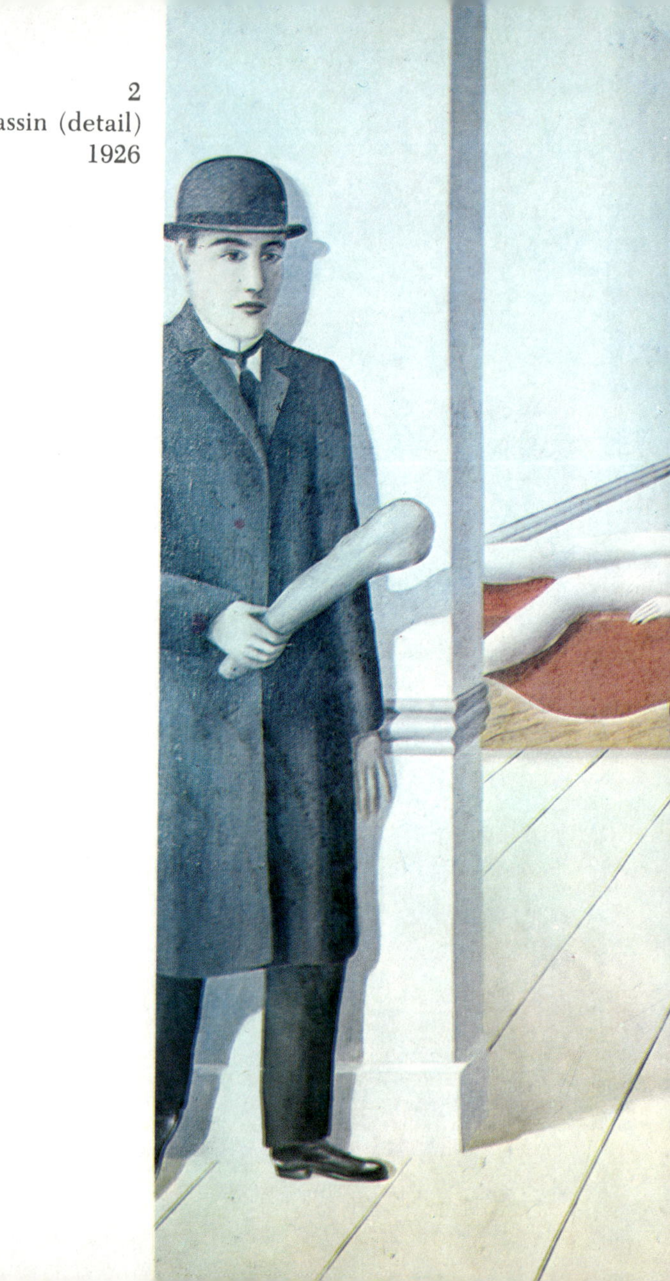

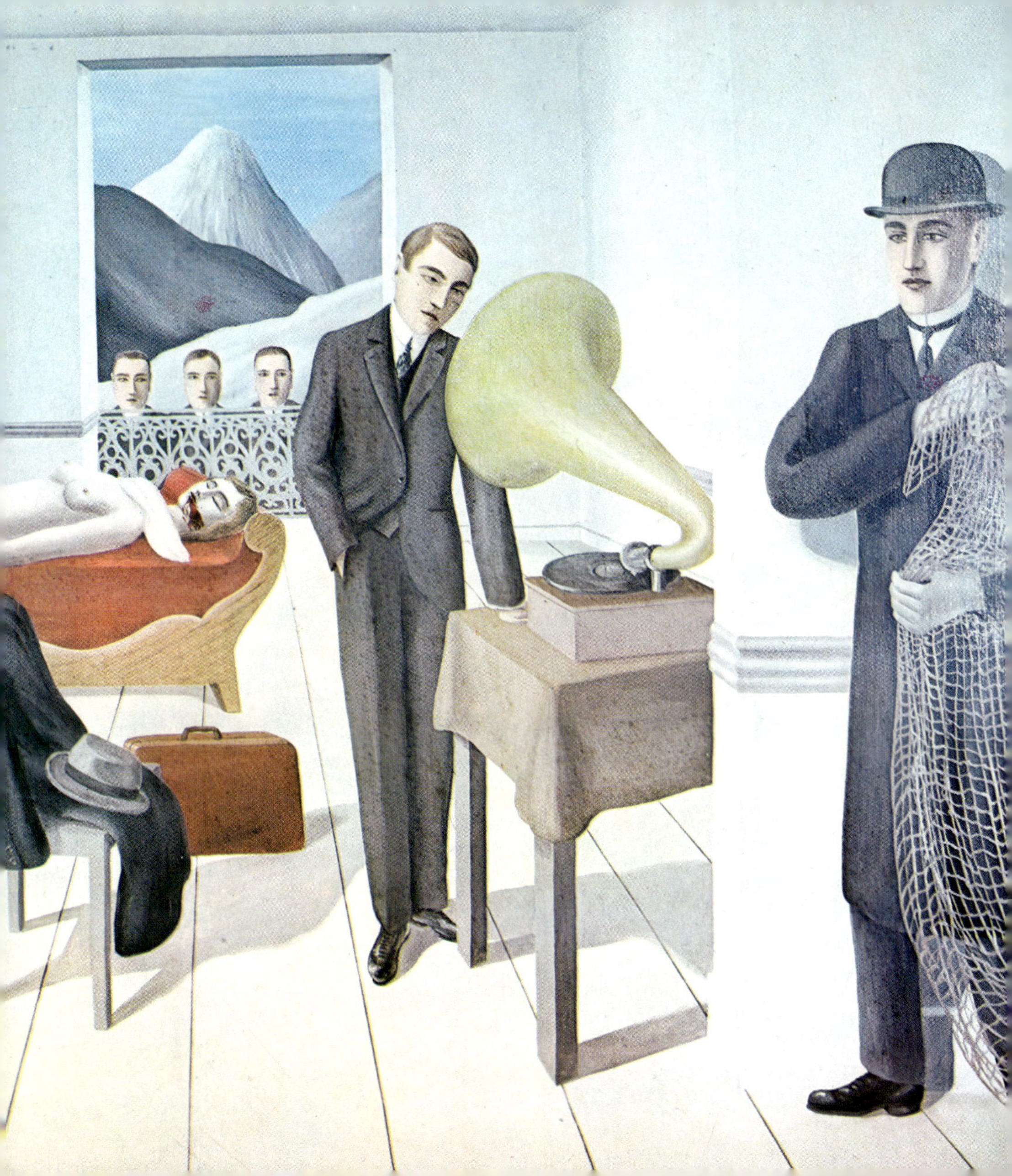

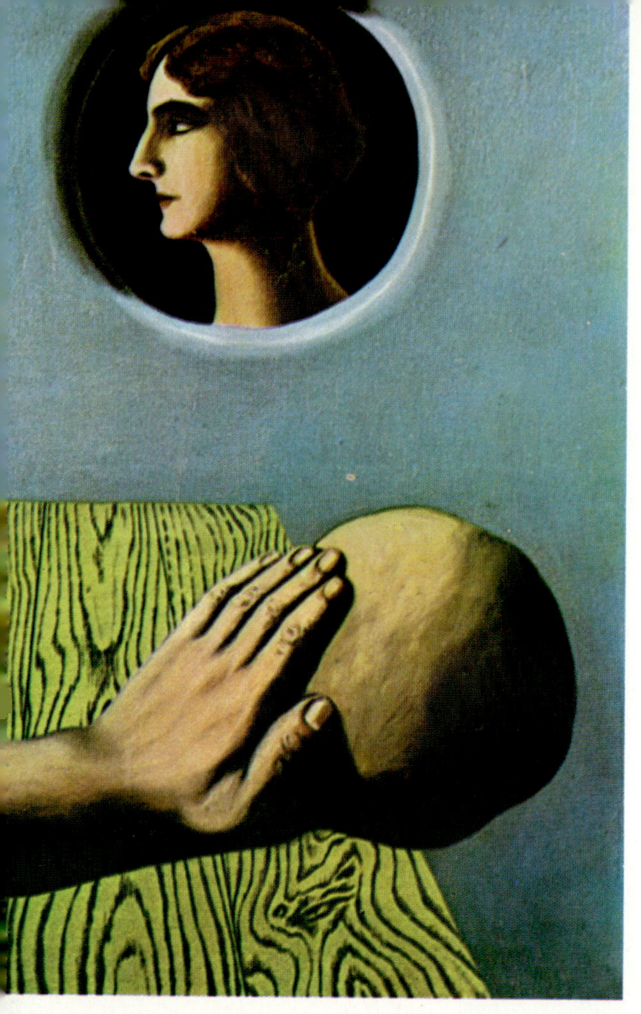

3
The salutary promise
1927

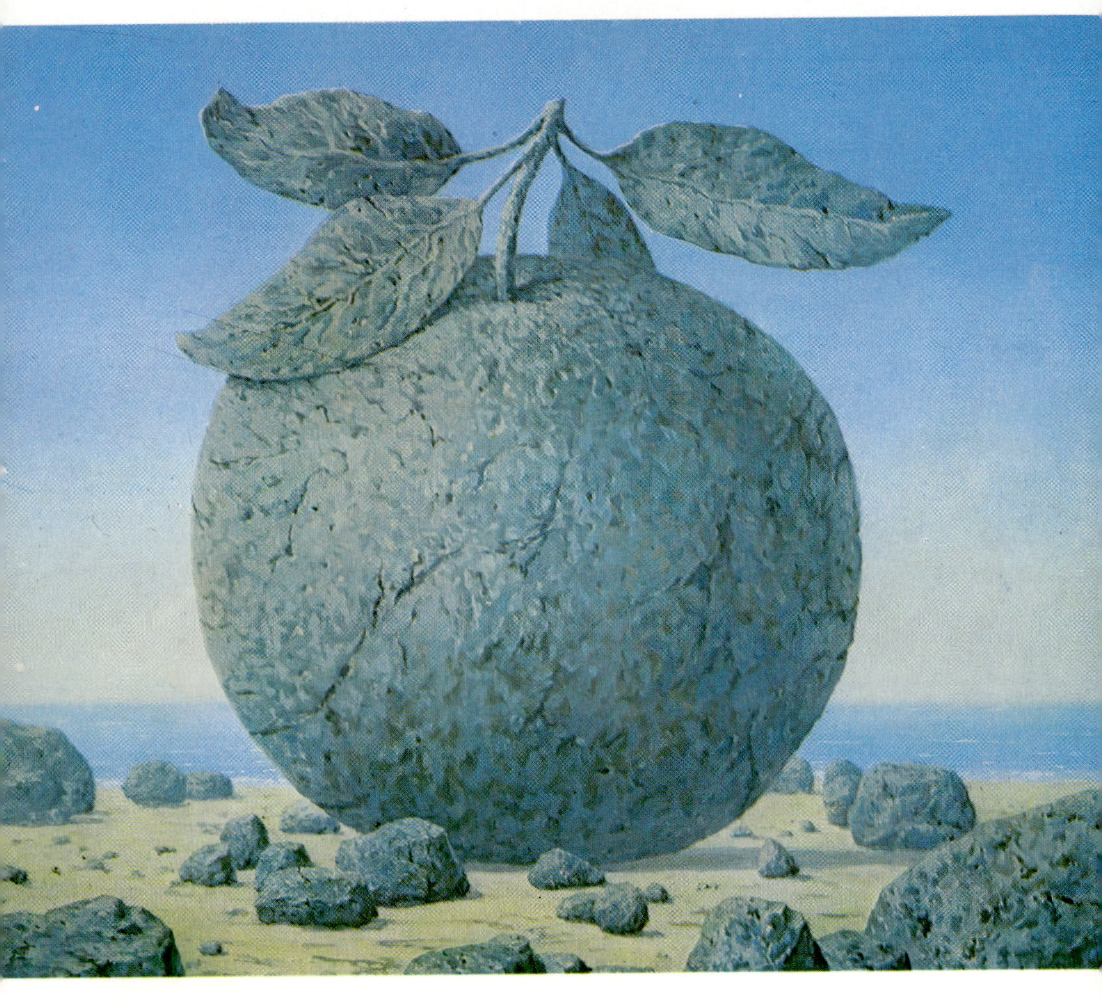

4
The large table
1958

5
The undiscoverable woman
1927

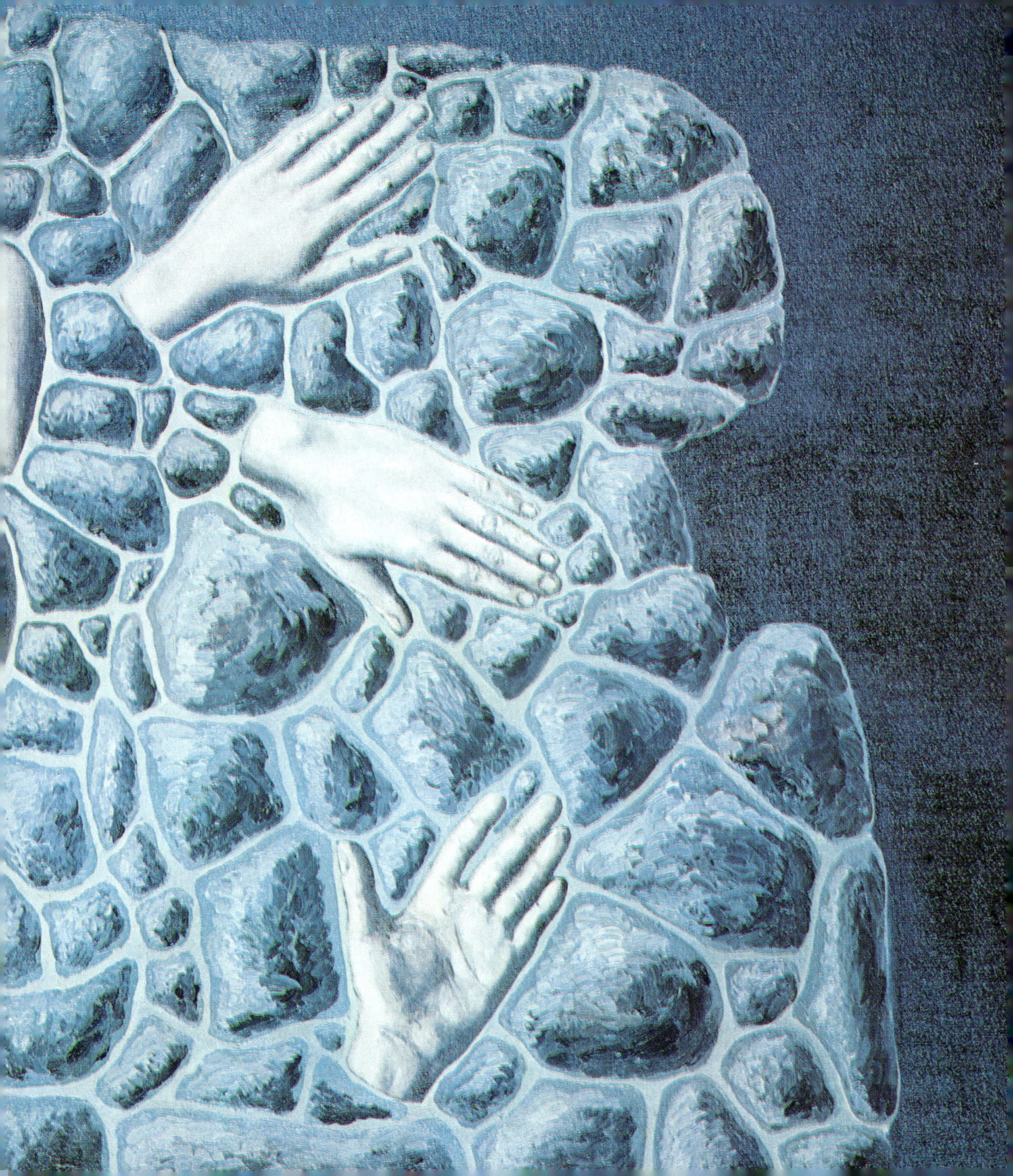

6
Personal values
1952

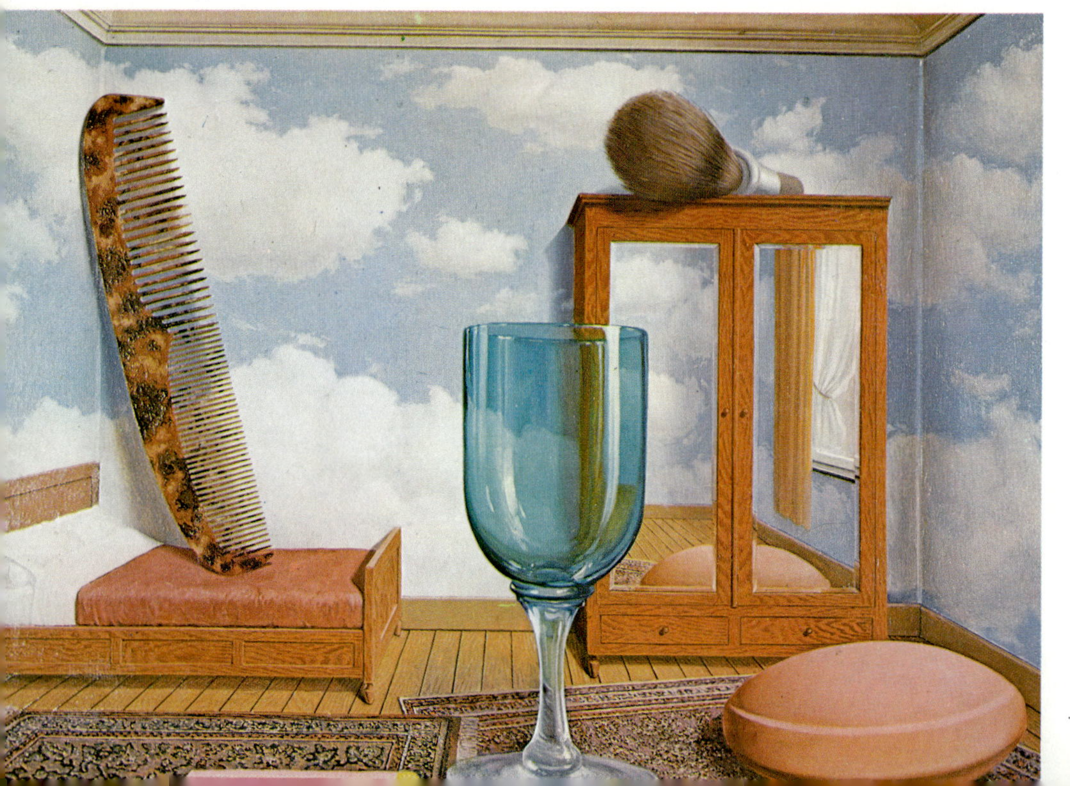

7
The gilt legend
1956

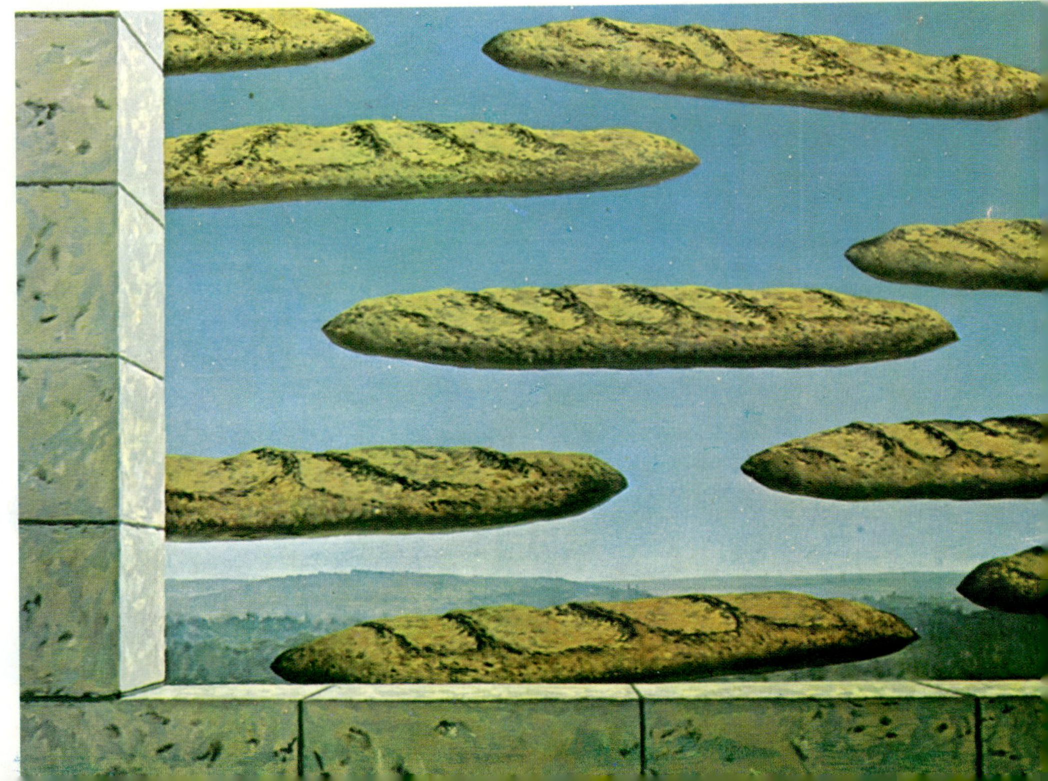

8
The trial of sleep
1926

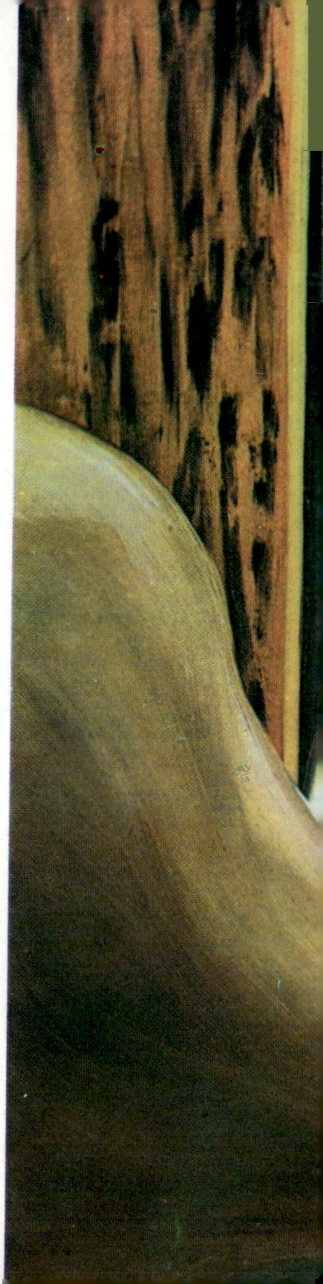

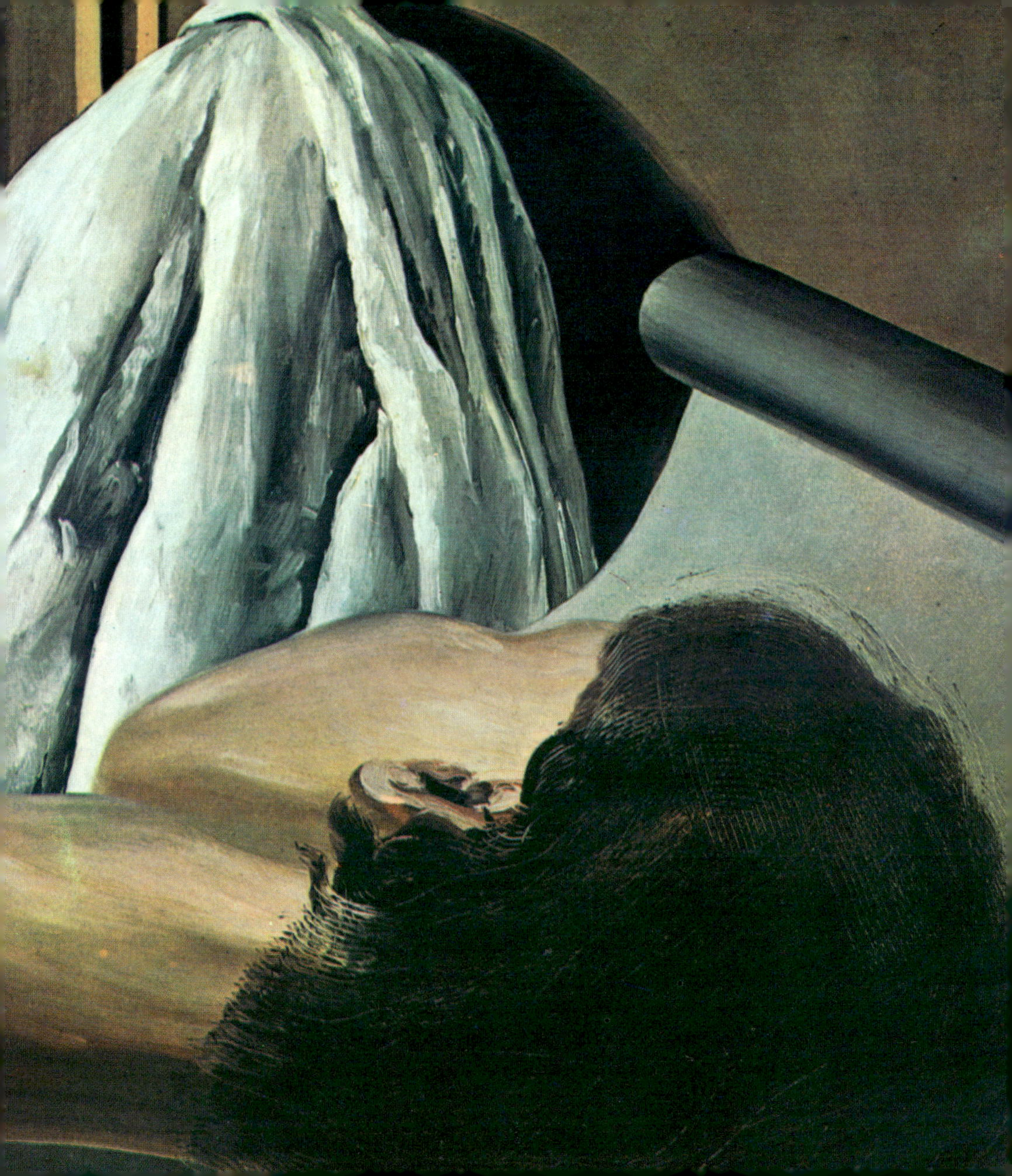

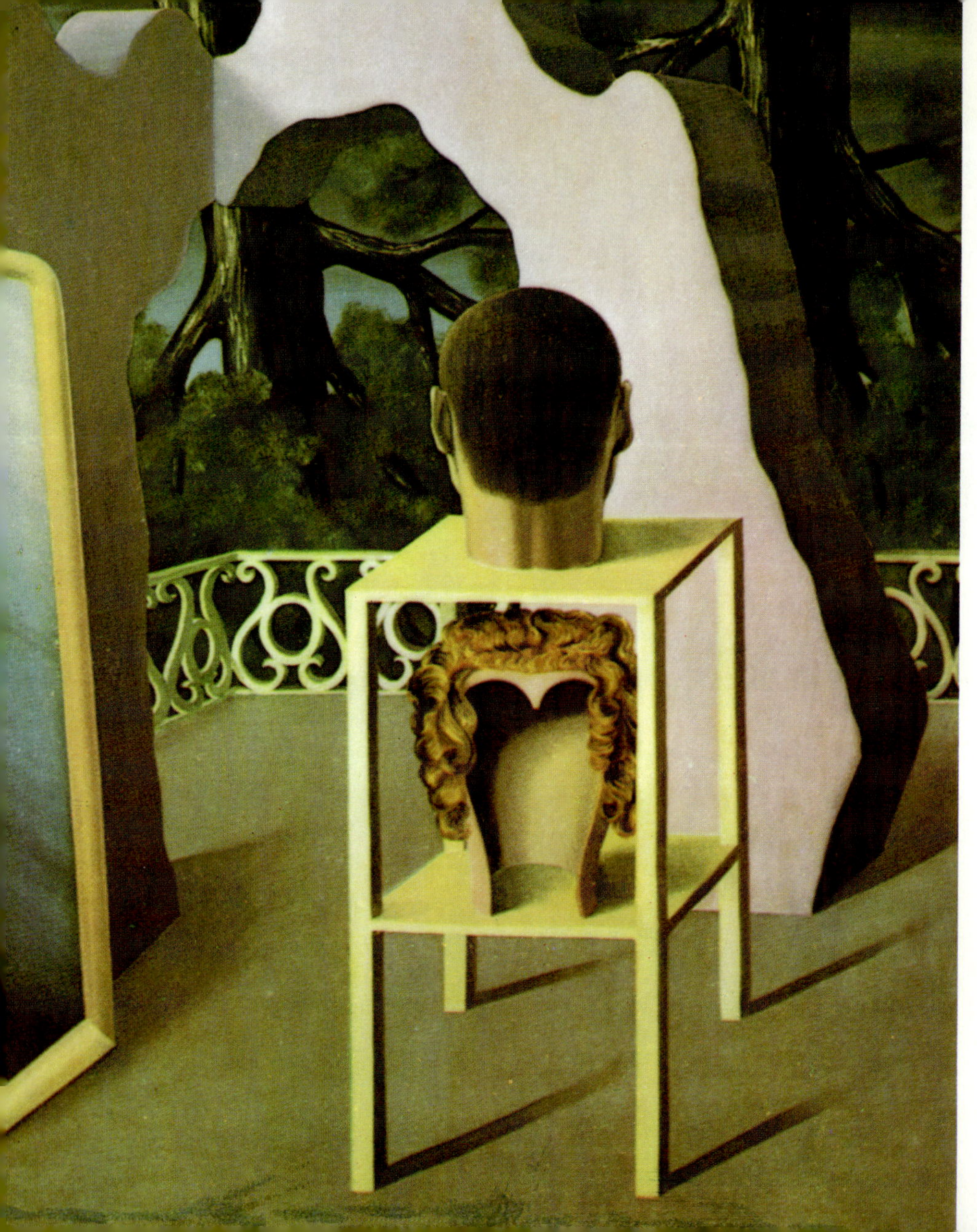

9
The marriage at midnight
1926

10
The inhabitants of the river
1926

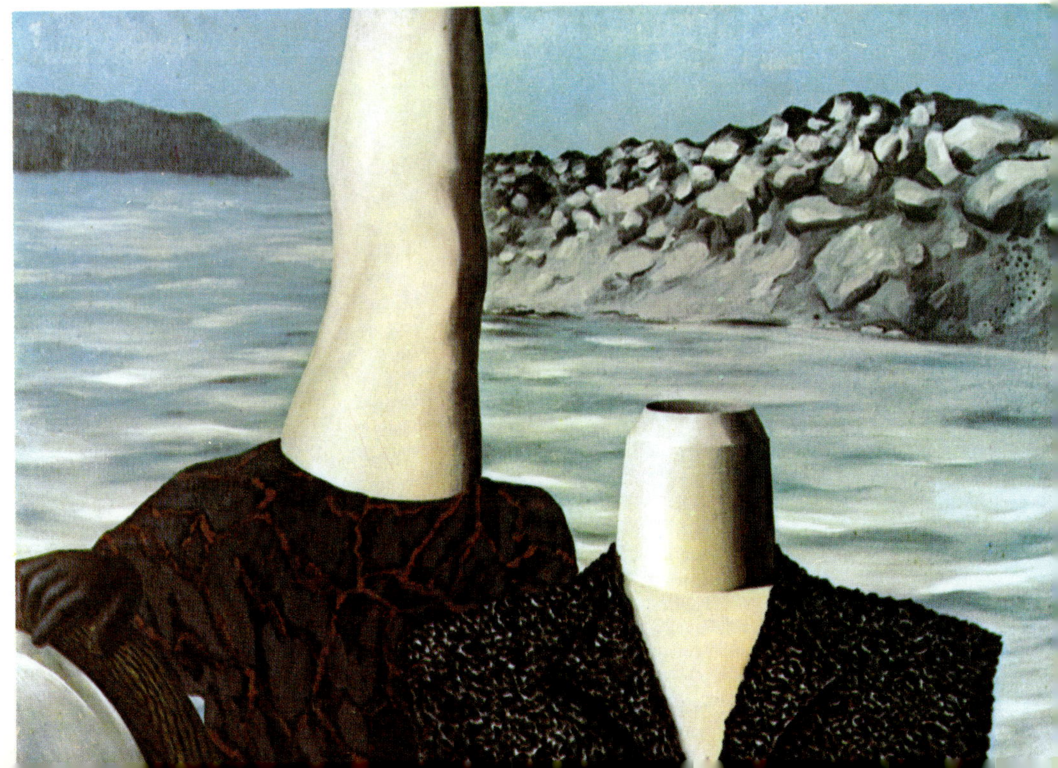

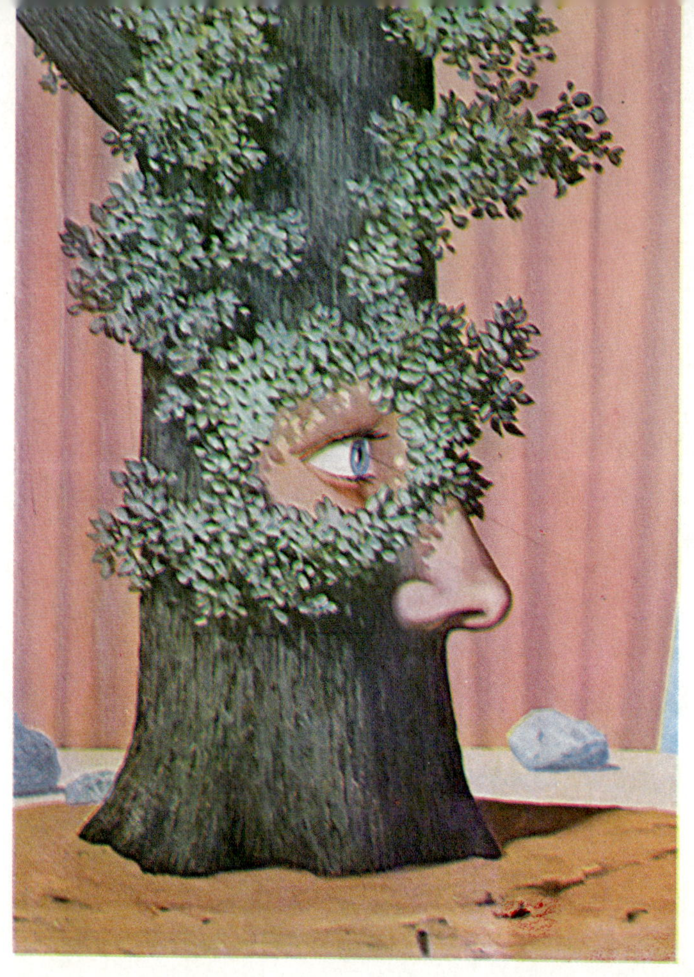

11
The enchanted domain (detail)
1952

12
The forest
1927

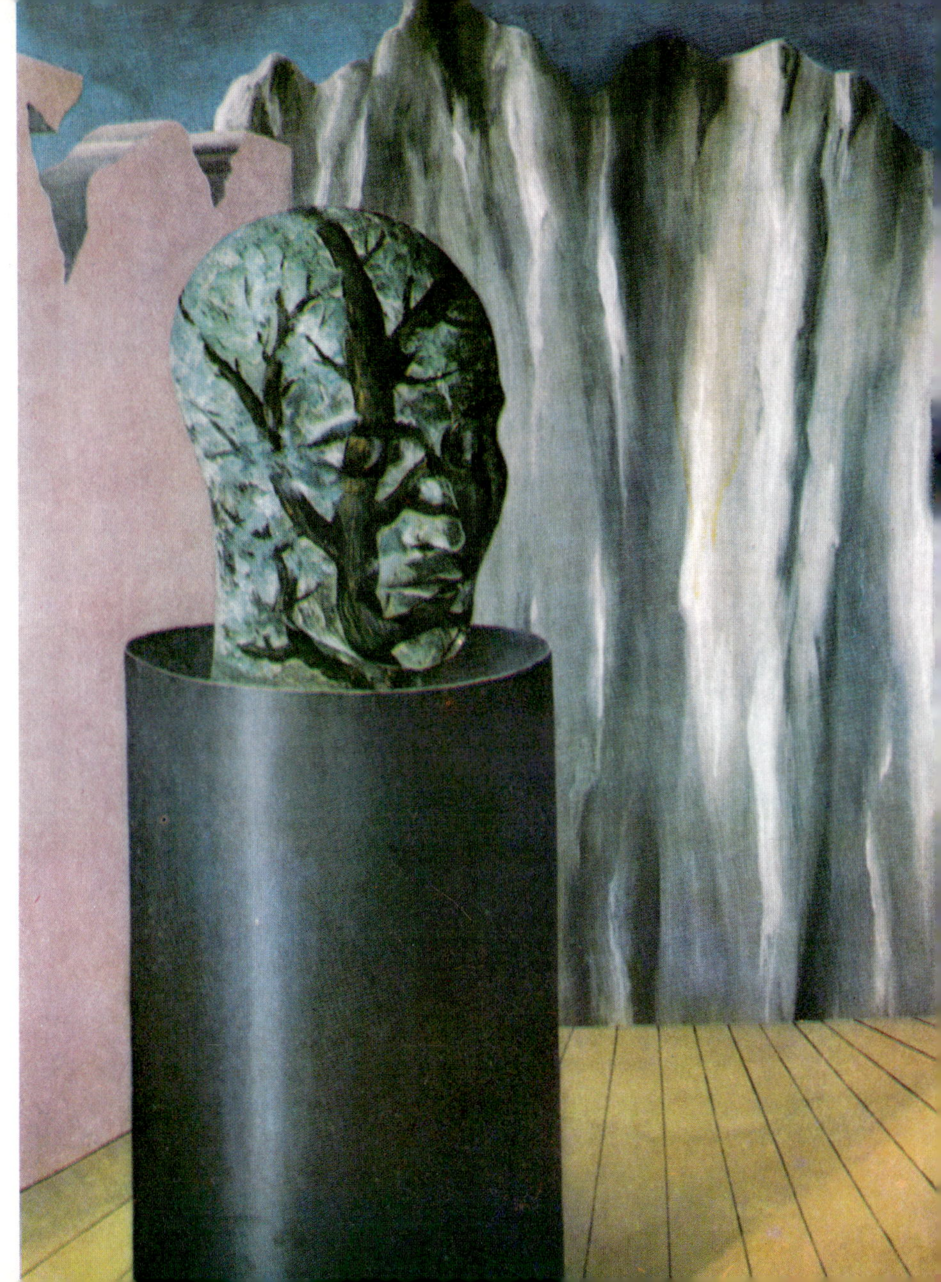

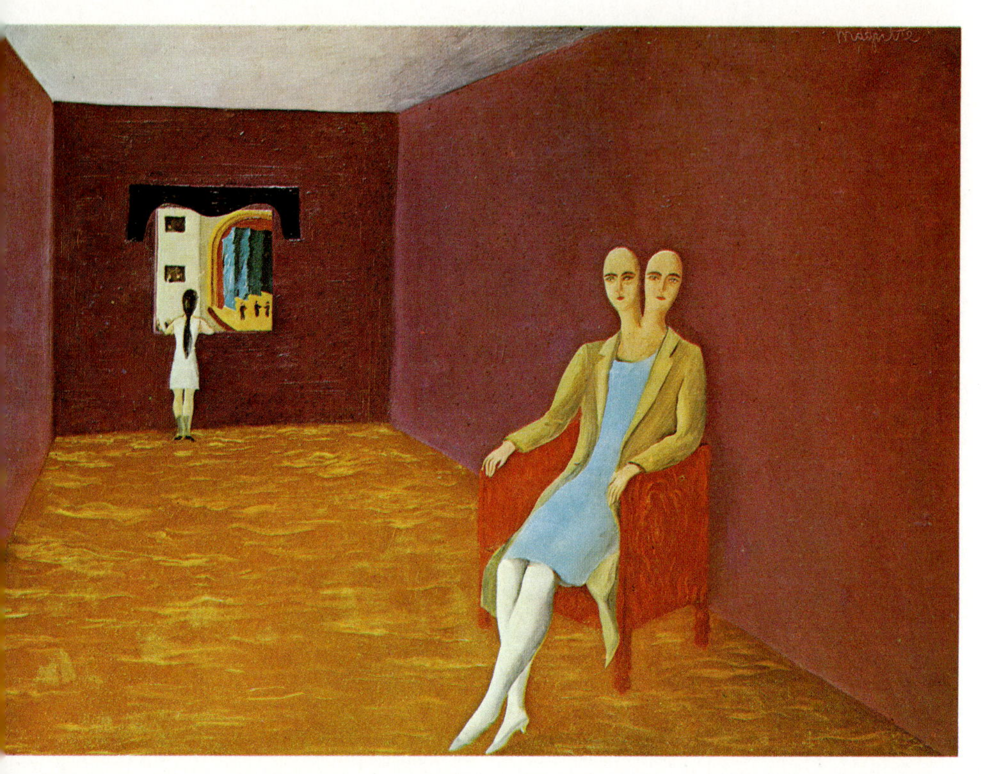

13
The stranger
1926

14
The commonplace

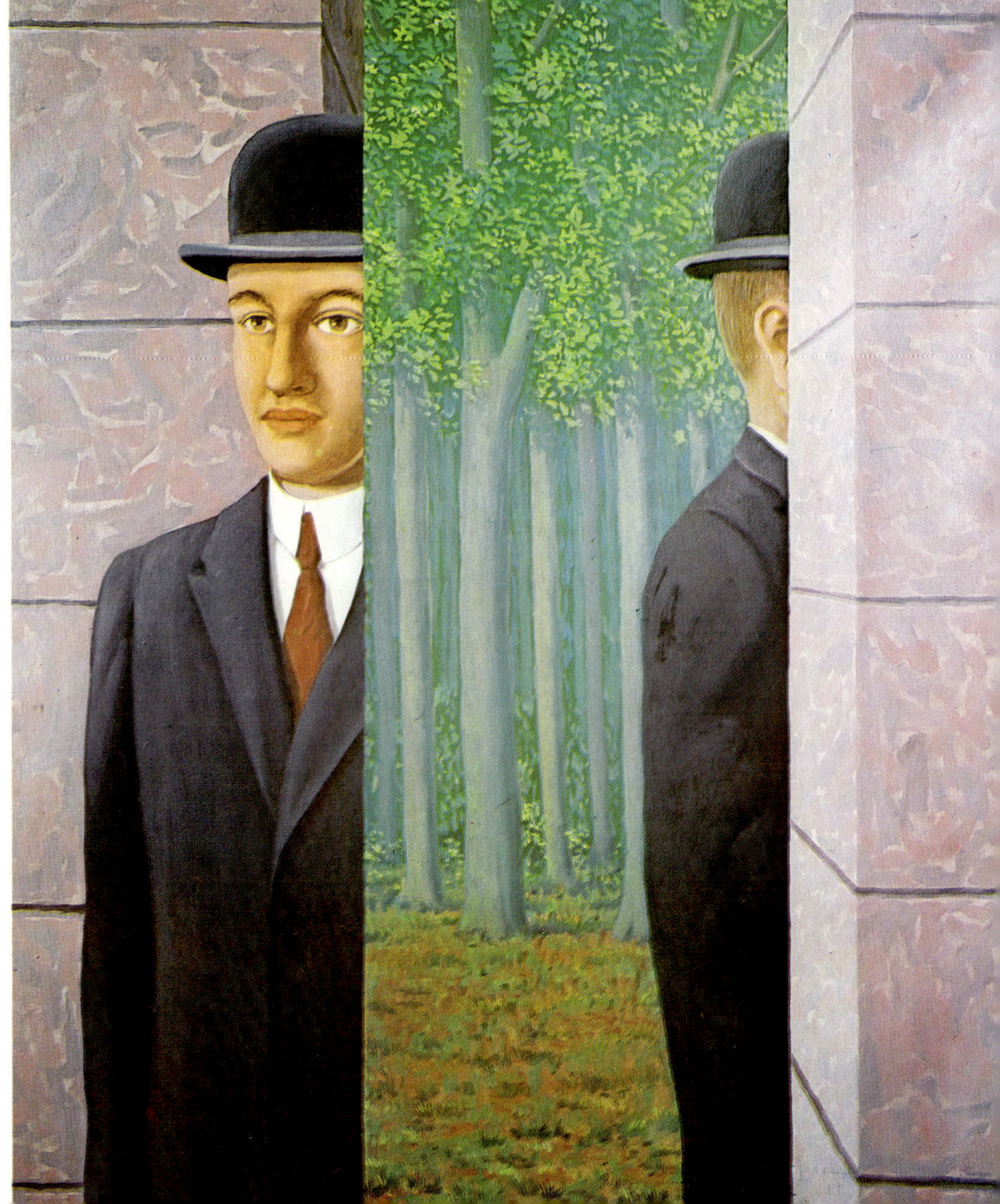

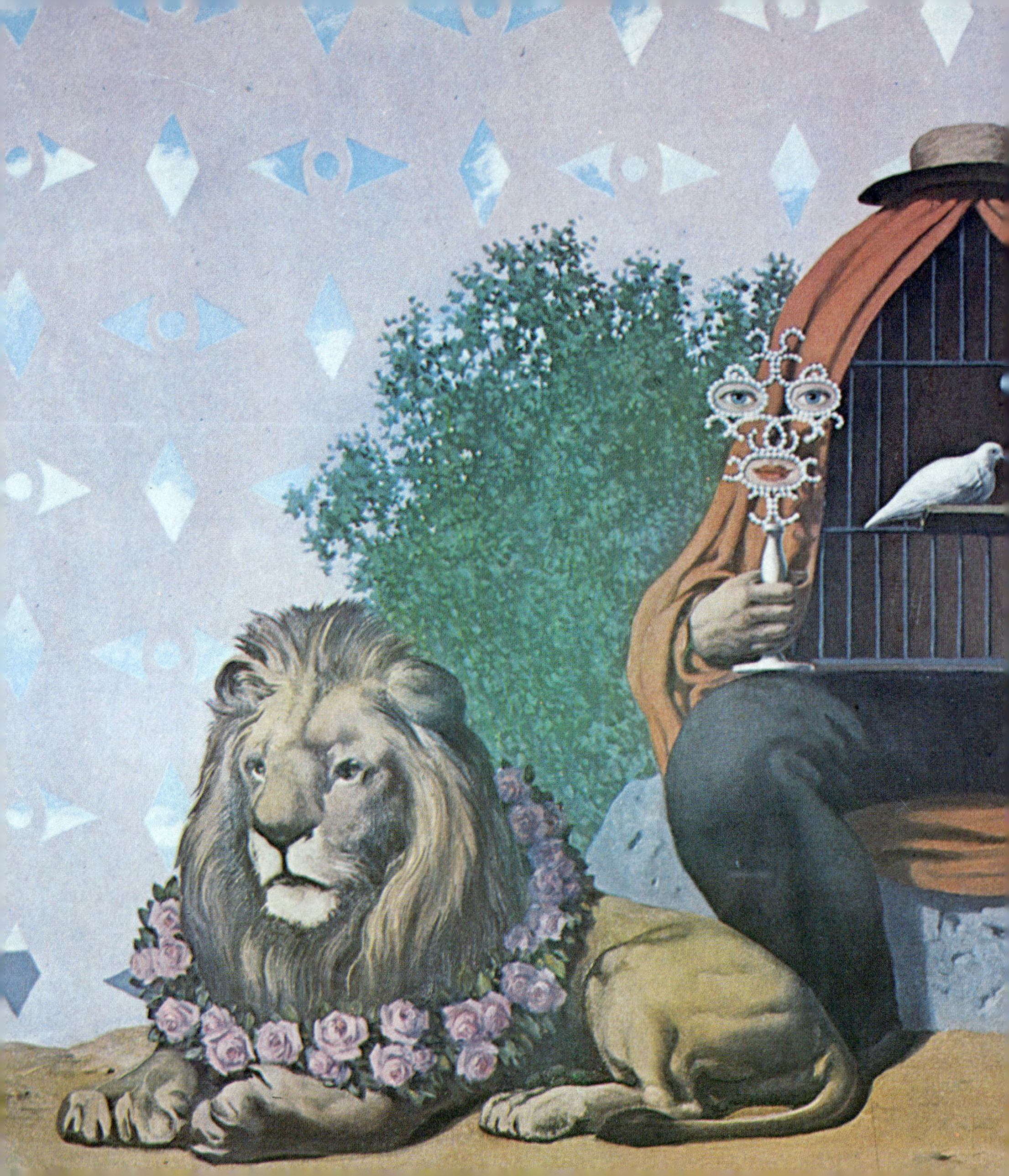

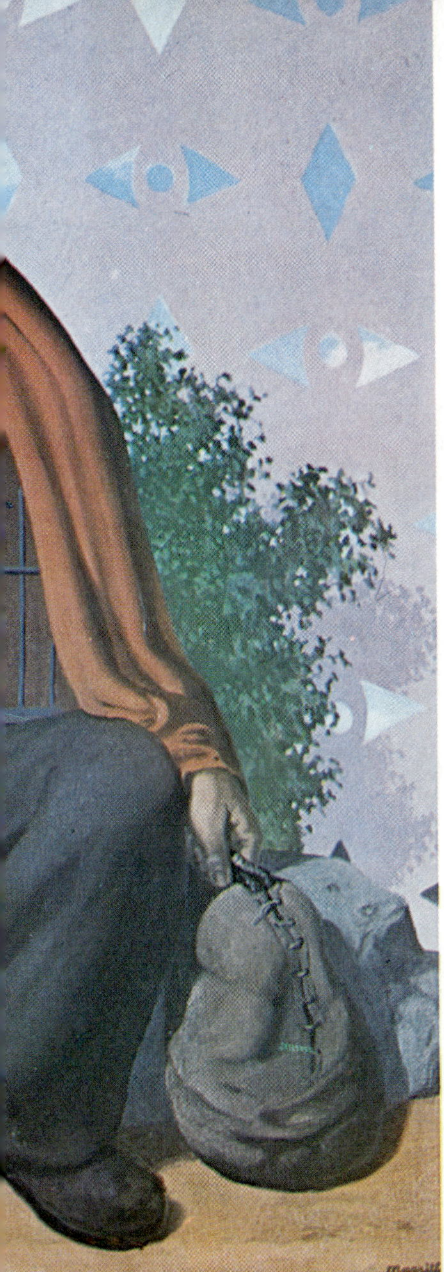

15
The enchanted domain
1952

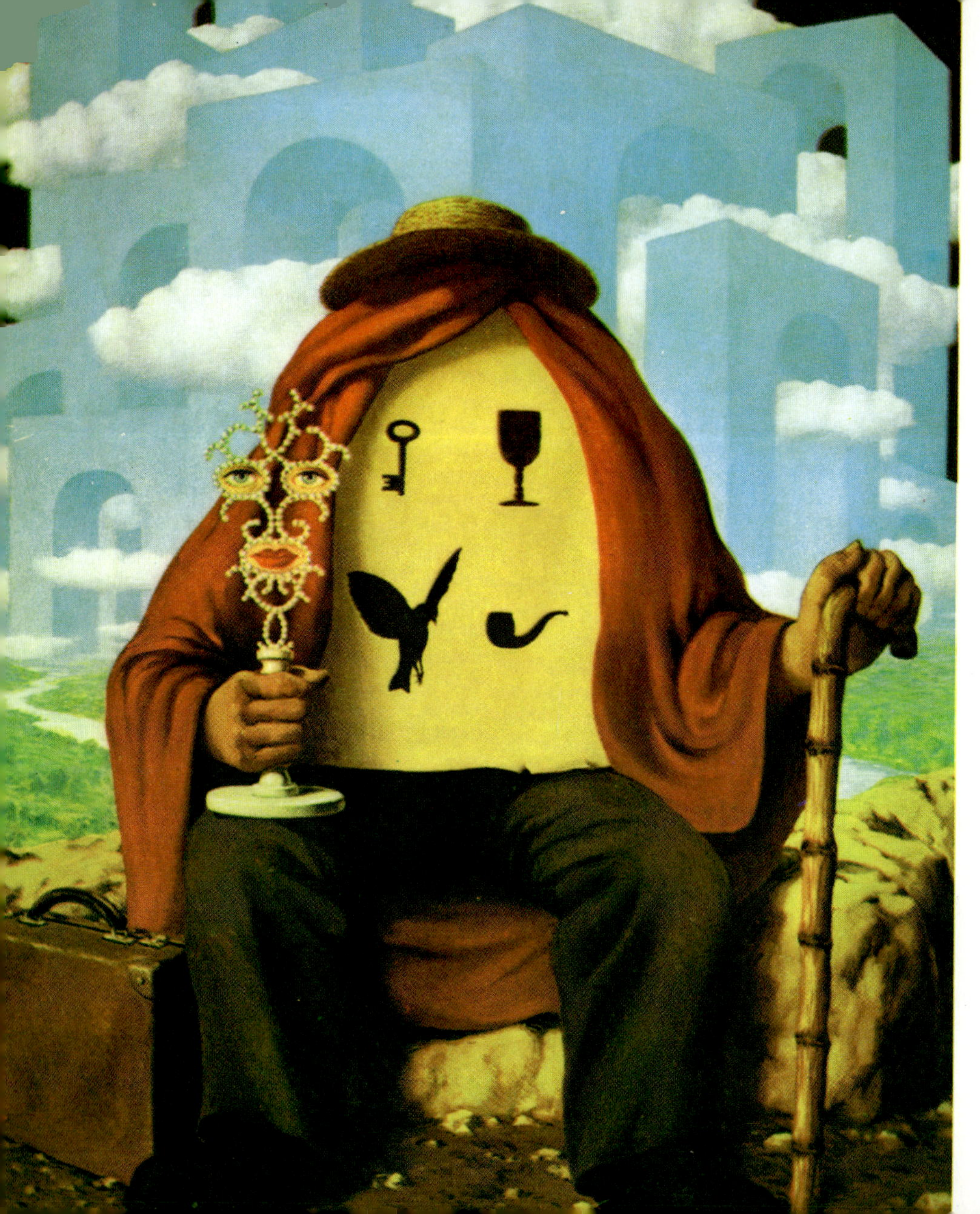

16
The liberator
1947

17
The therapeutist
1937

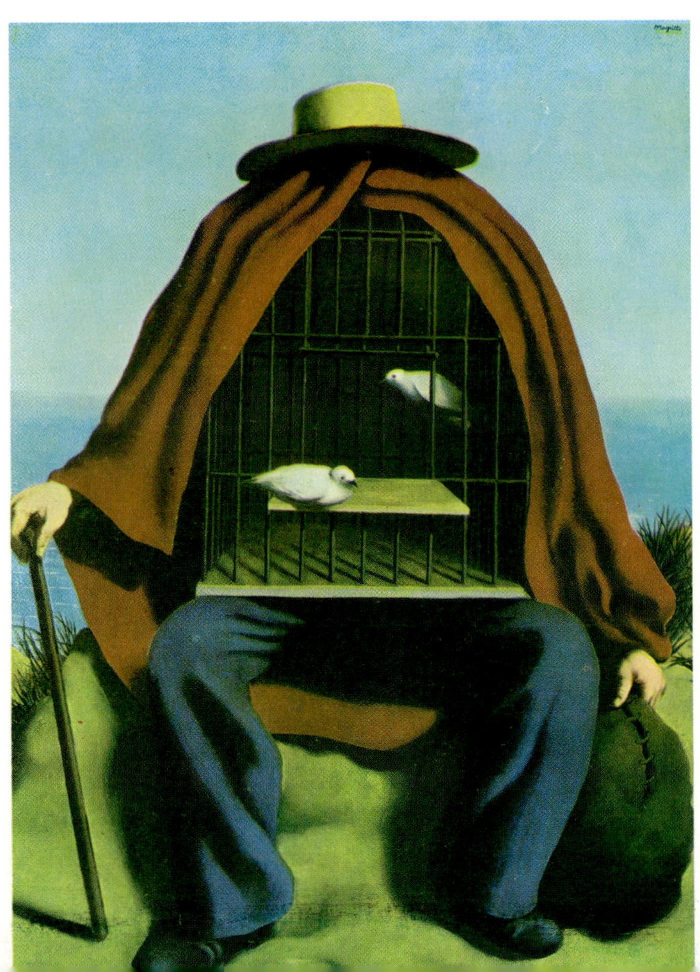

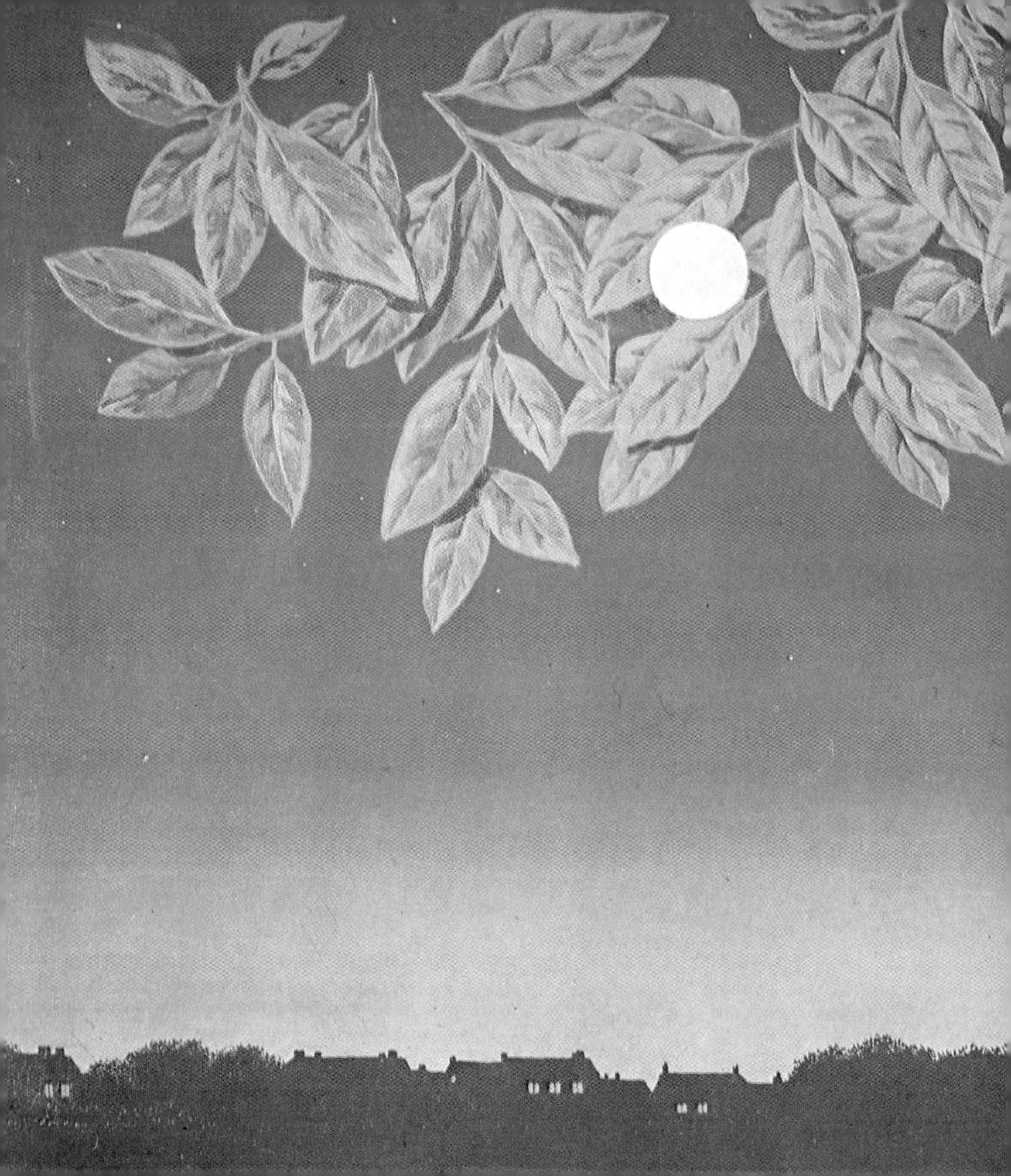

18
The blank page

19
The empire of lights
1958

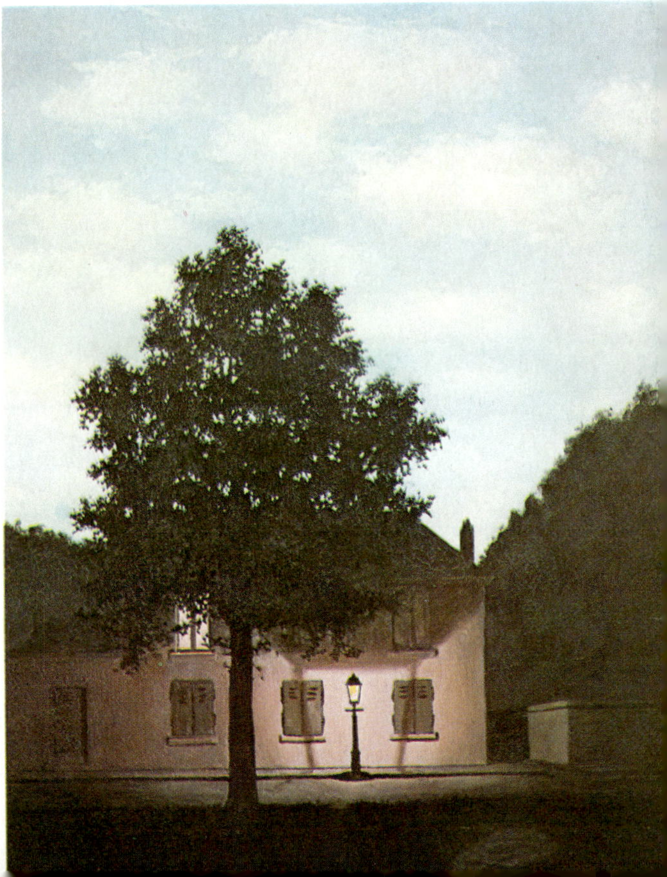

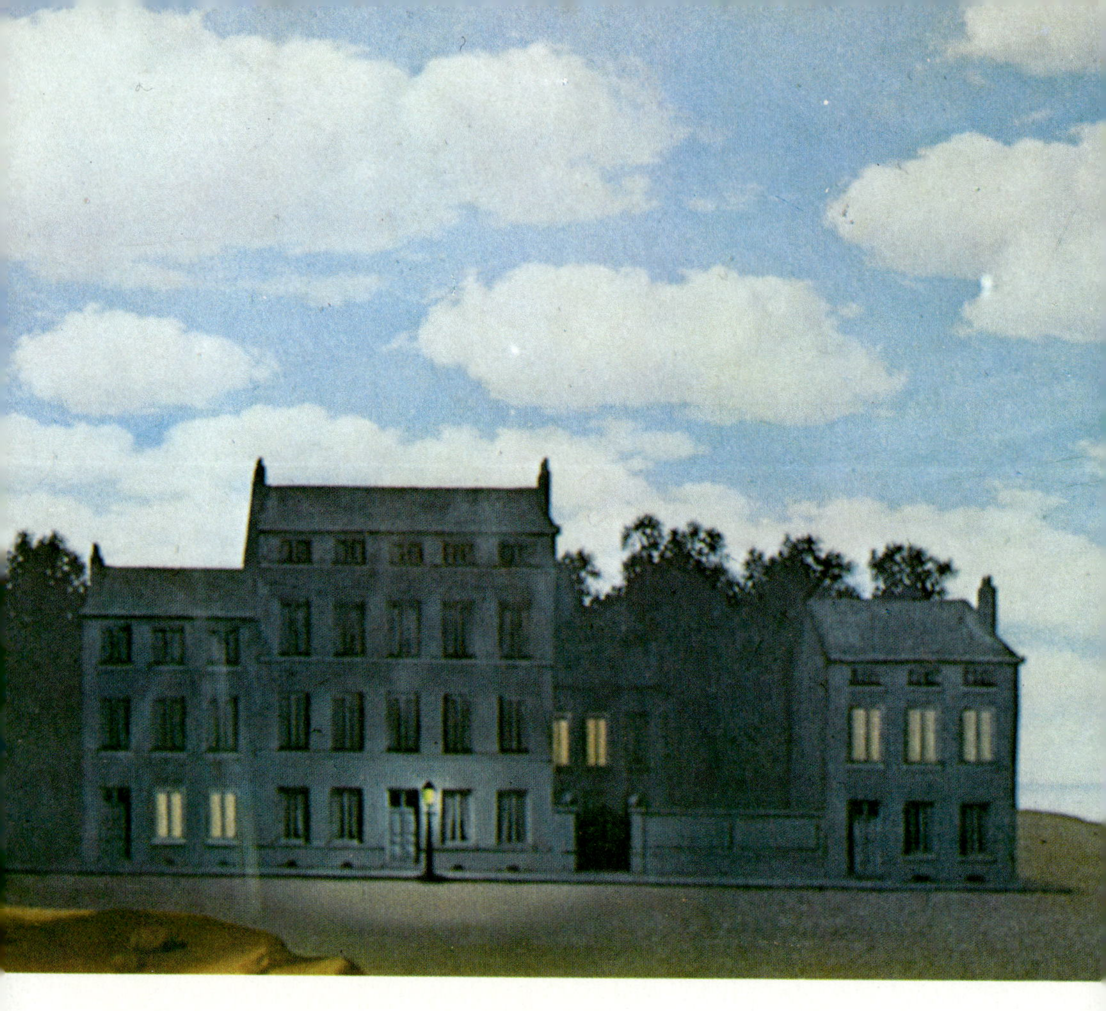

20
The enchanted domain (detail)
1952

21
The empire of lights
1954

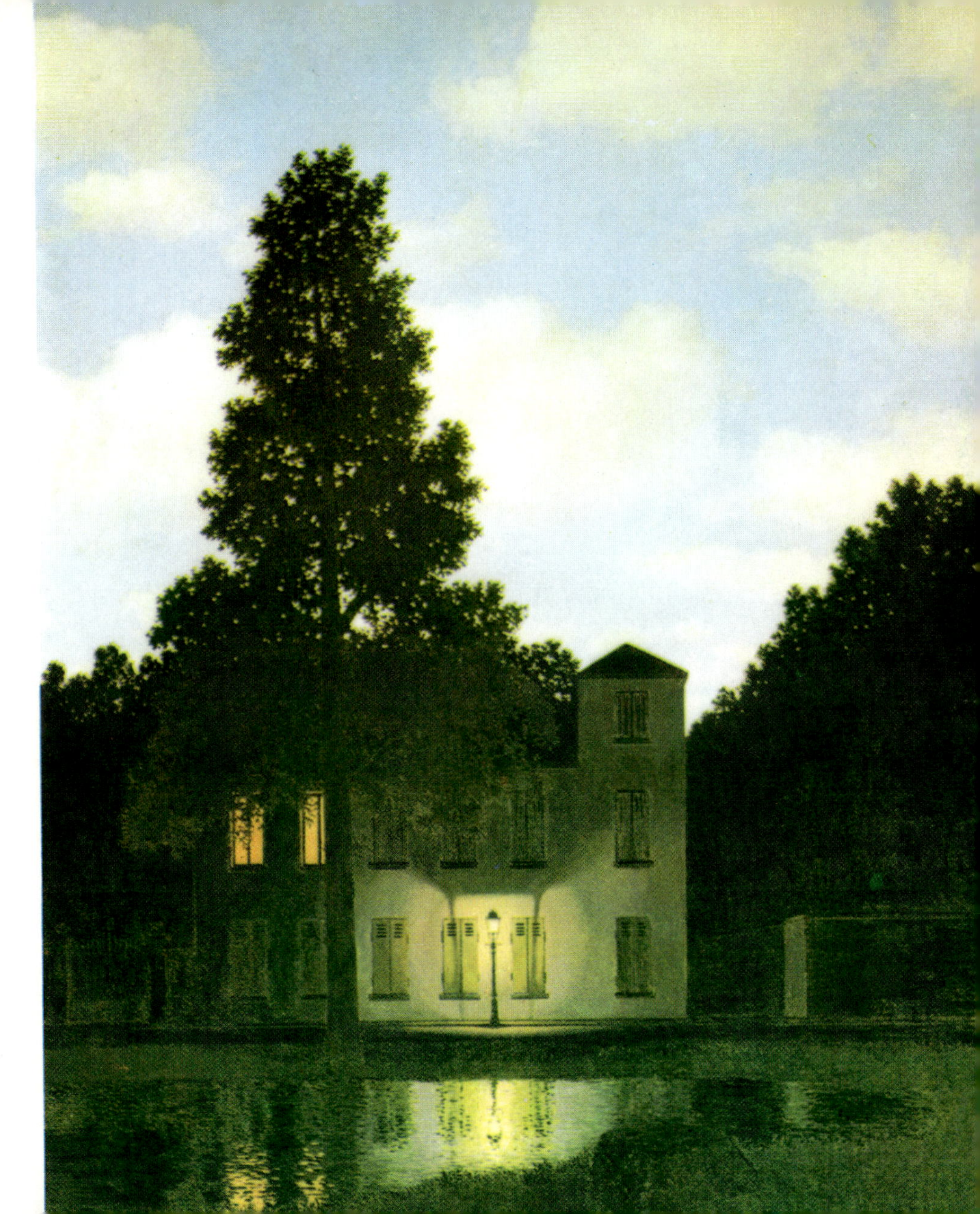

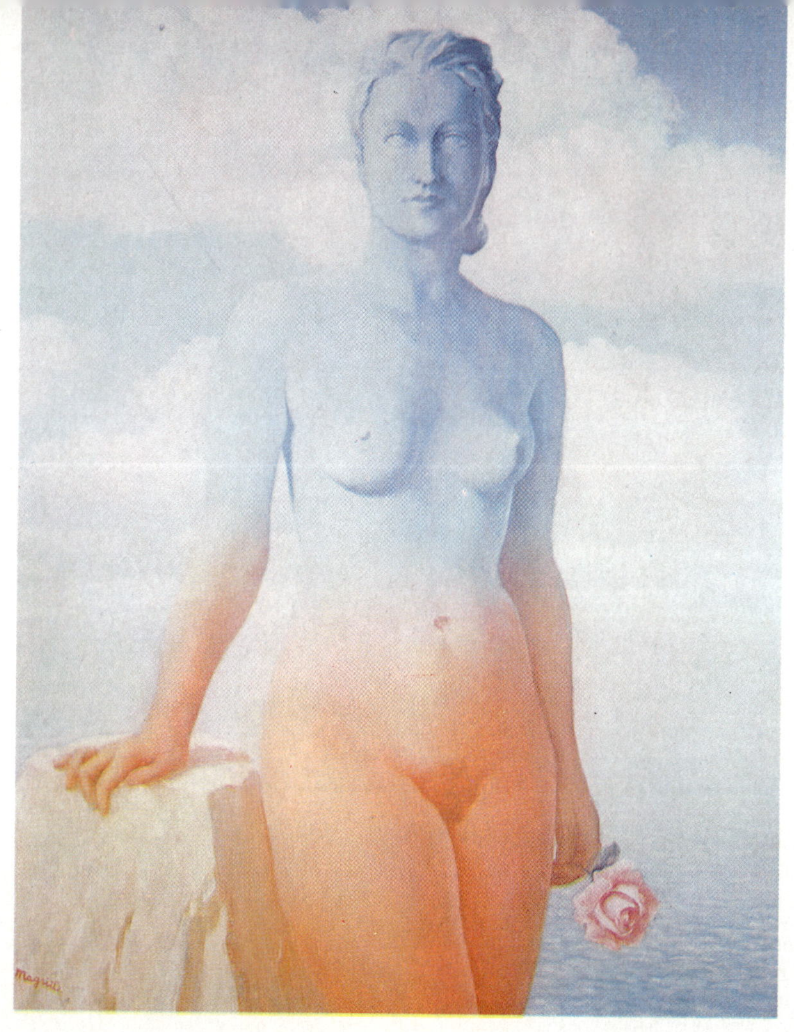

22
Woman with a rose

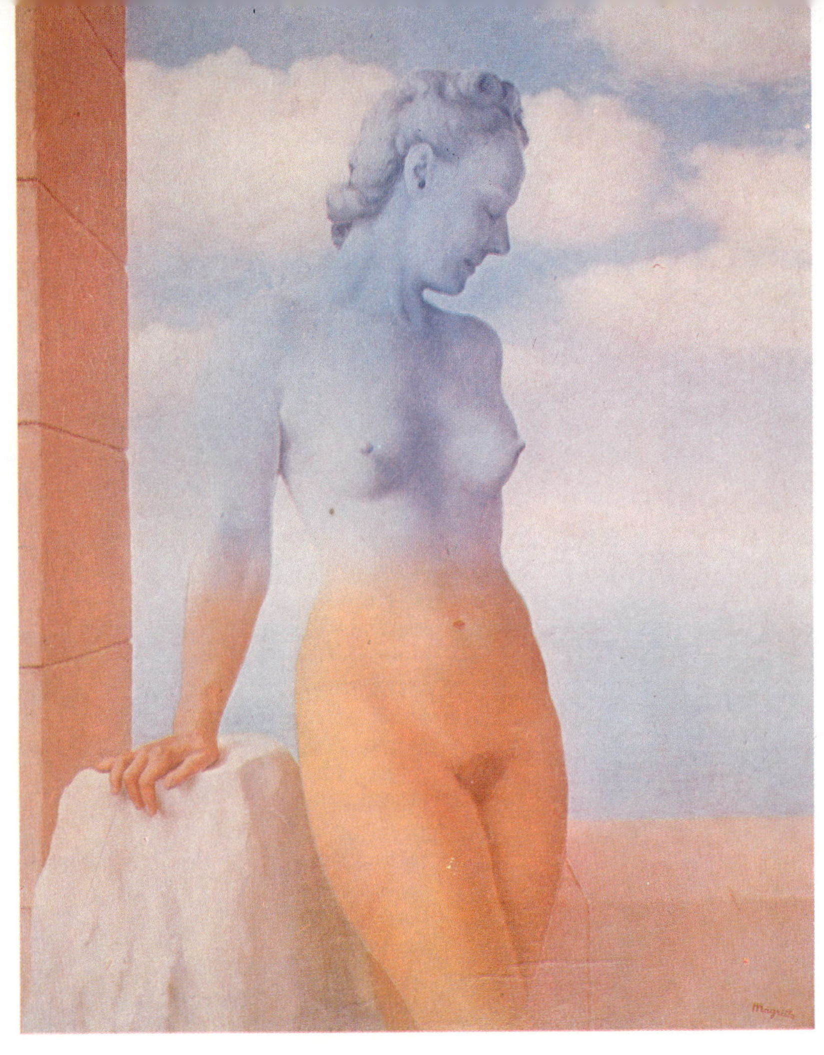

23
Black magic

24
The enchanted domain
1952

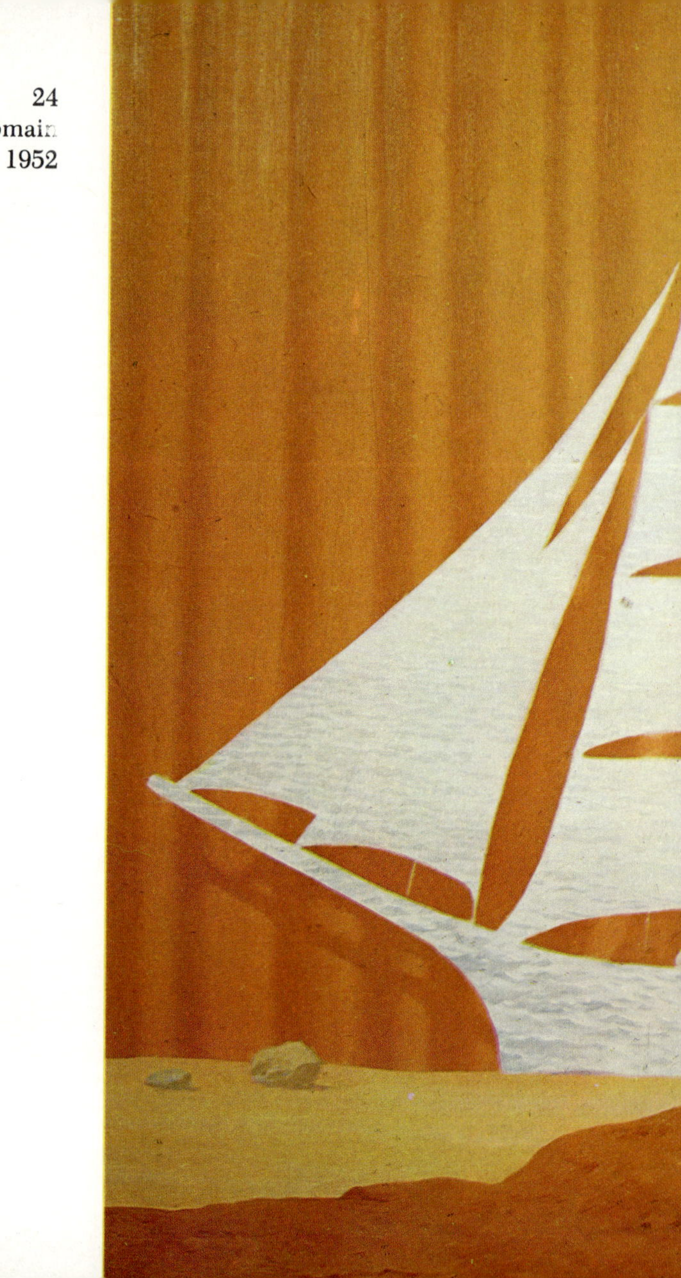

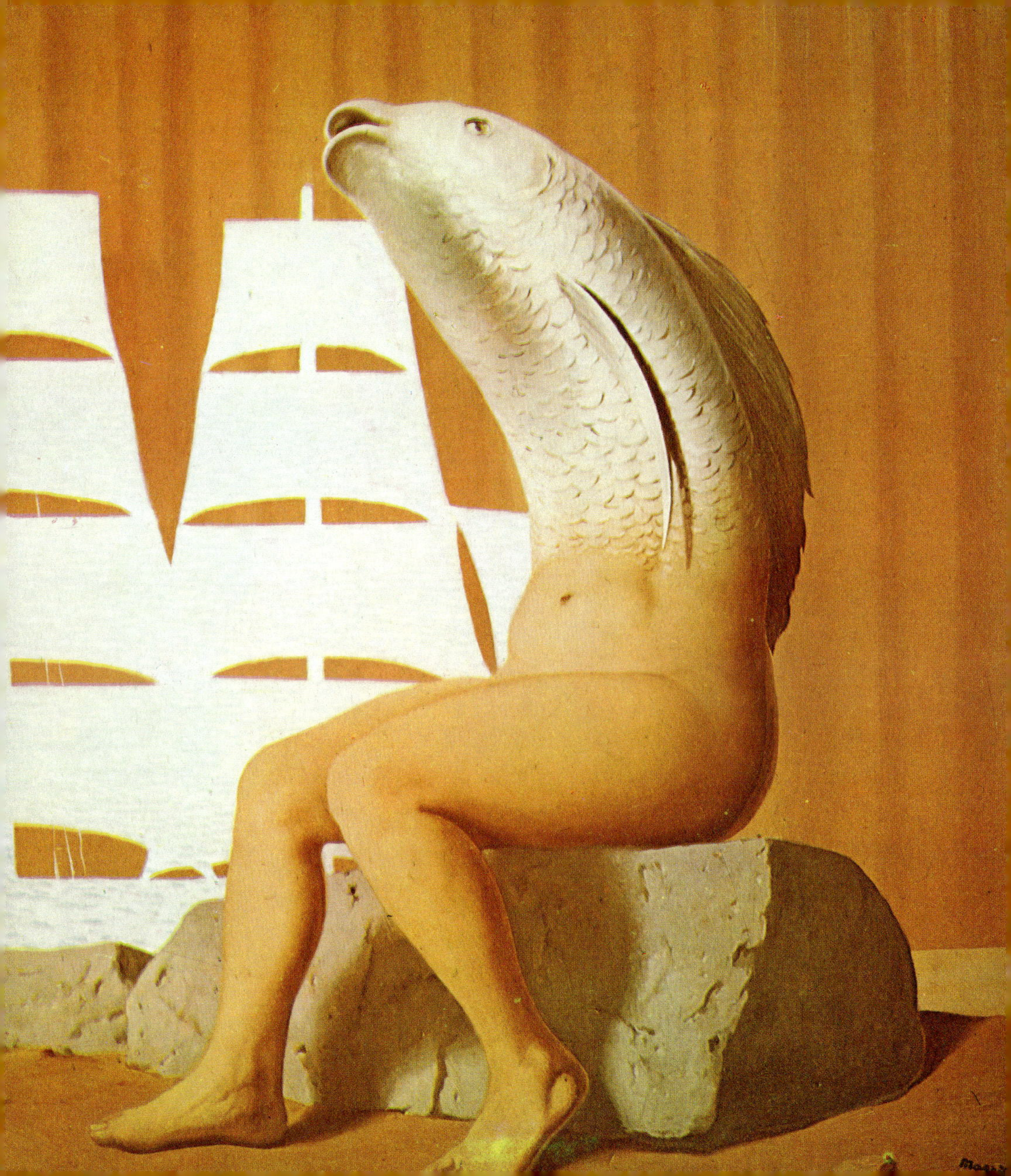

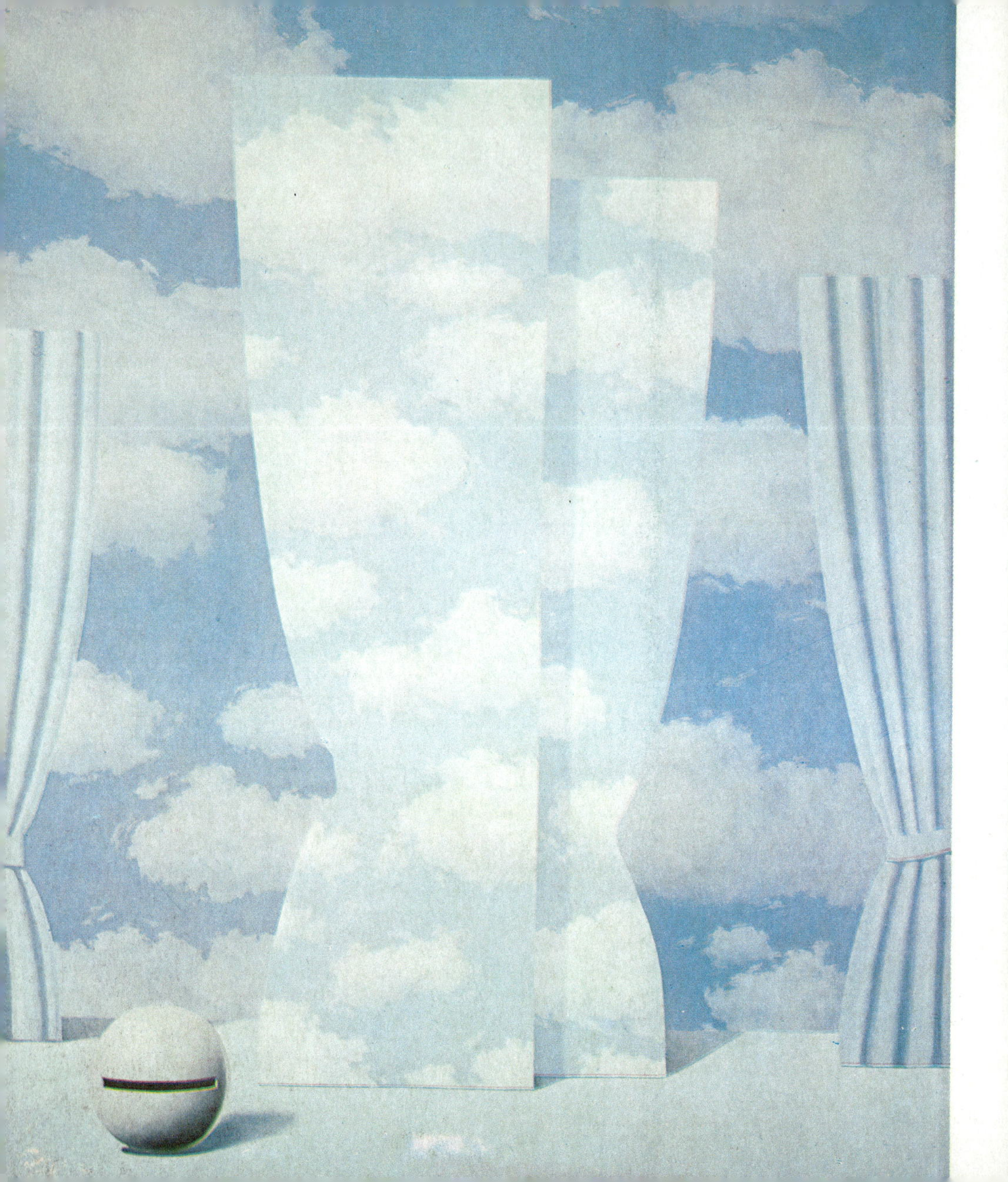

25
The lost pain

26
Good company
1950

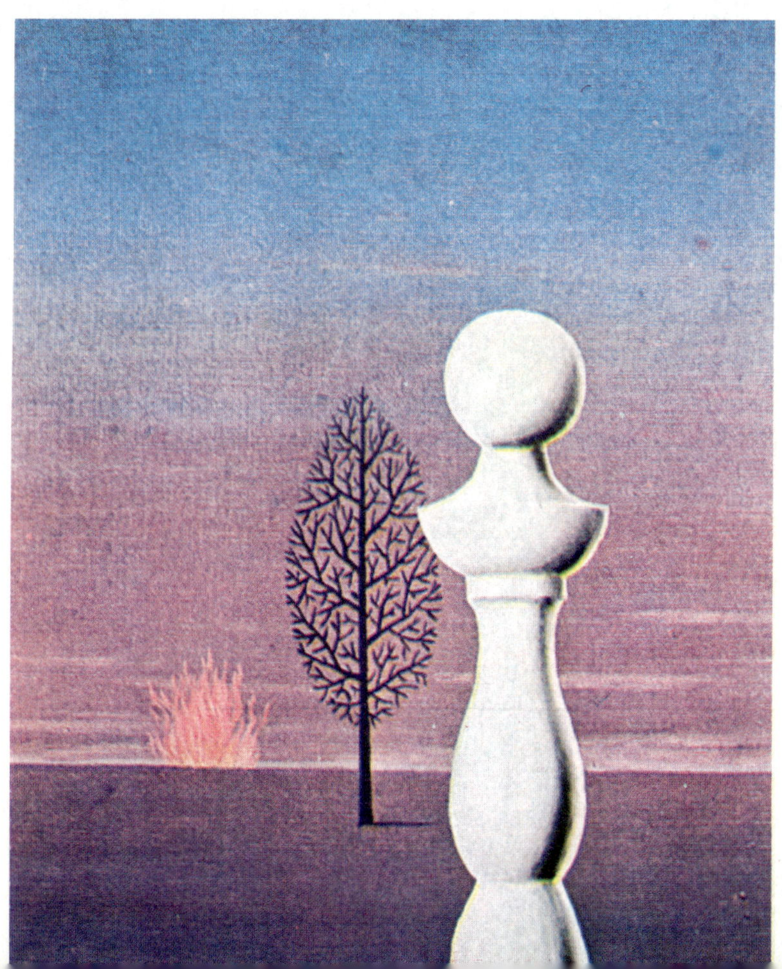

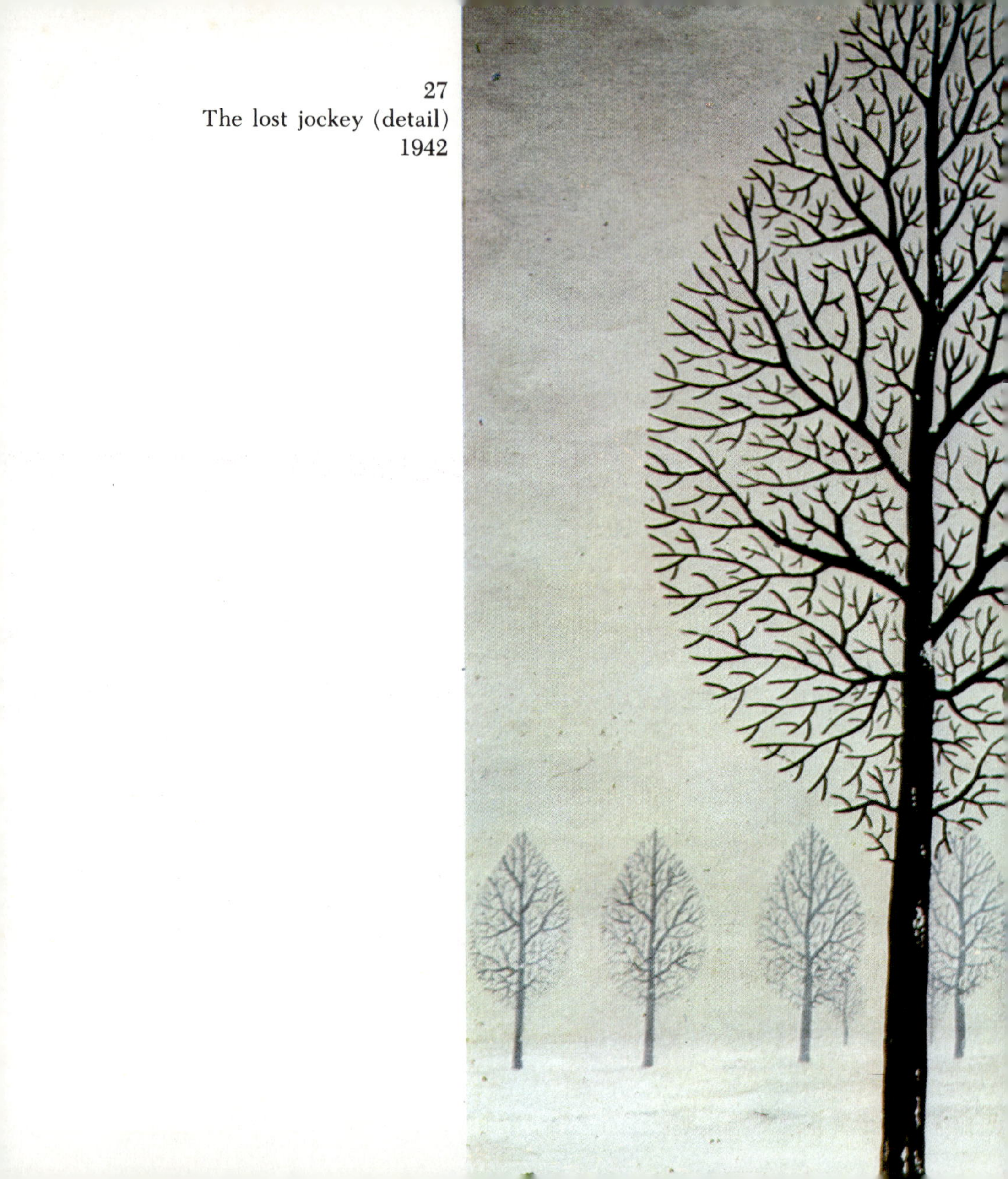

27
The lost jockey (detail)
1942

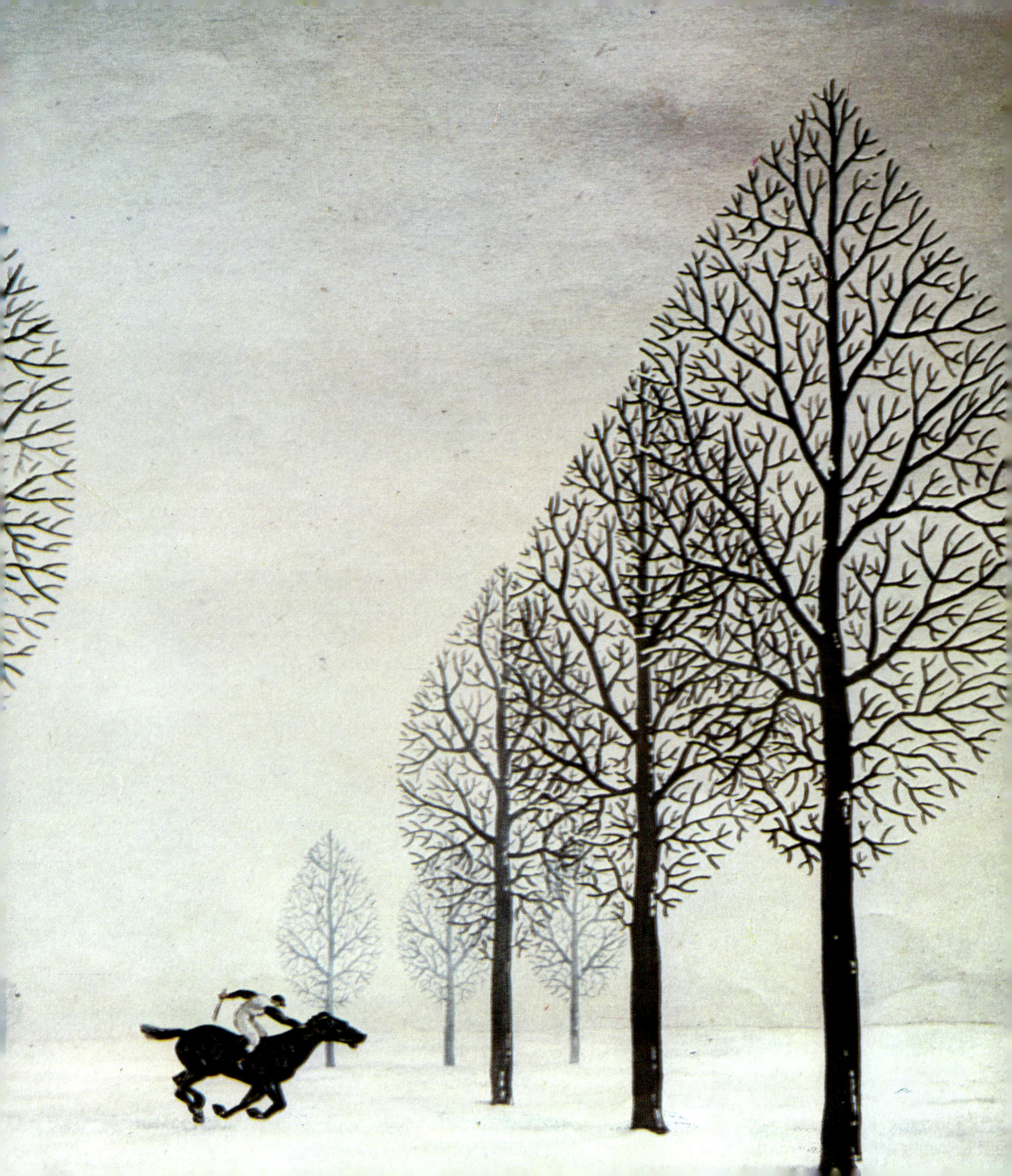

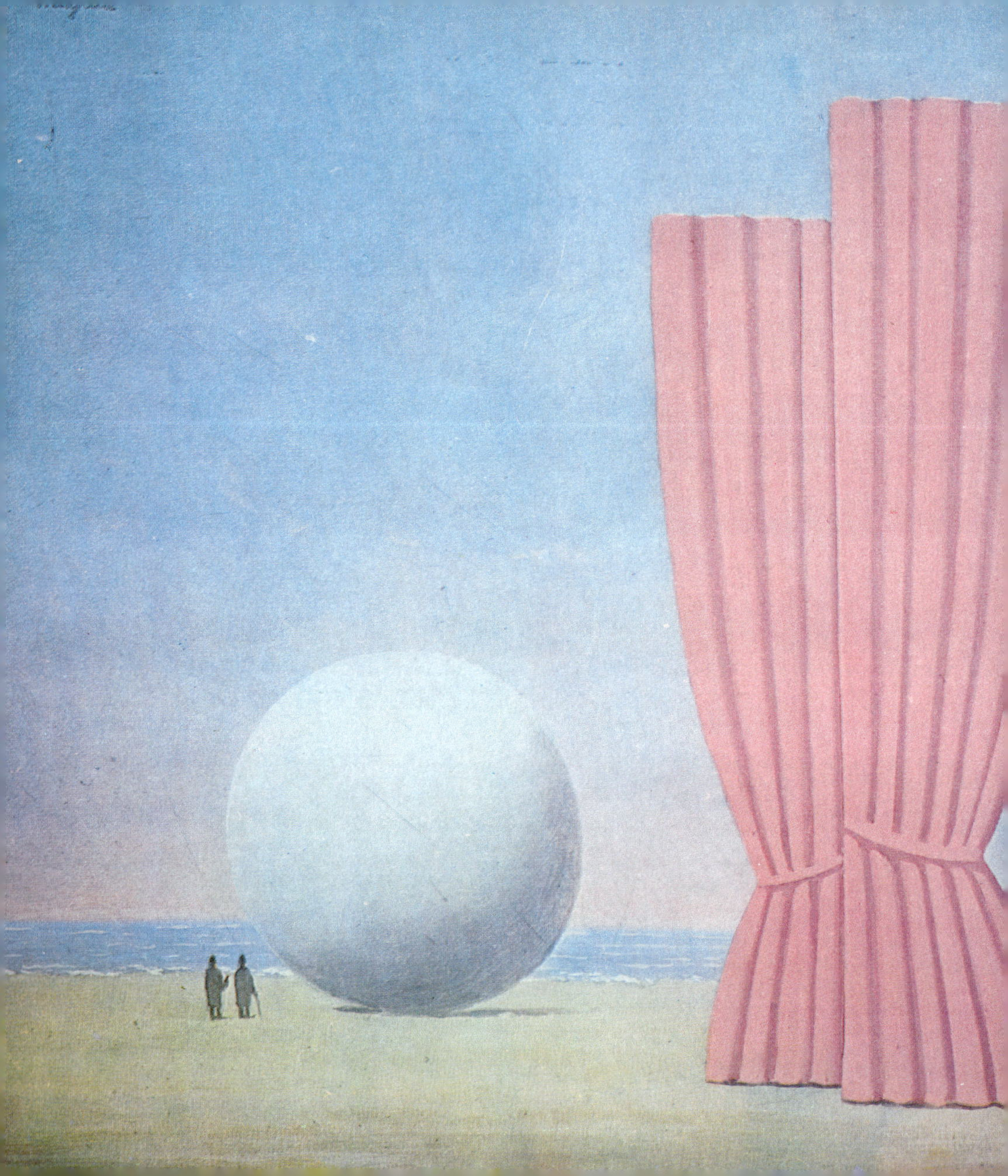

28
The awakened world (detail)
1958

29
Infinite gratitude
1963

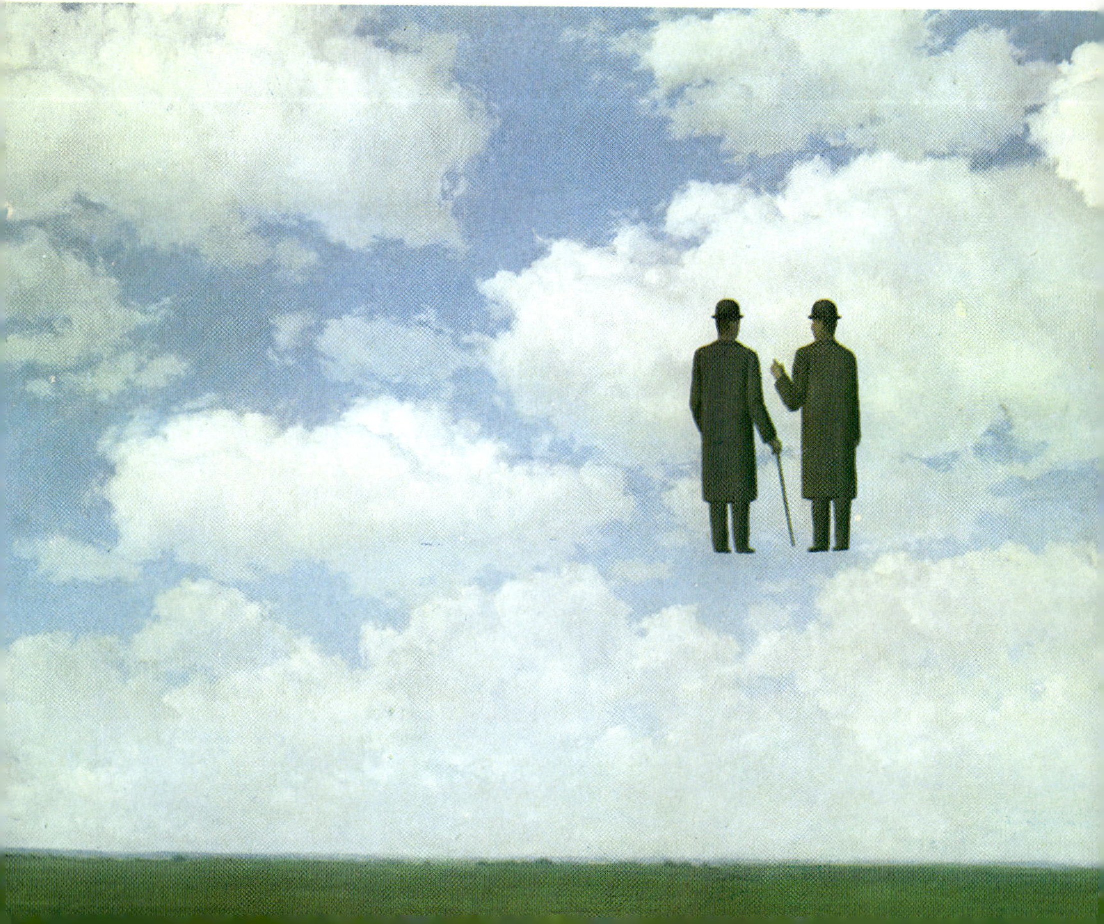

30
Untitled

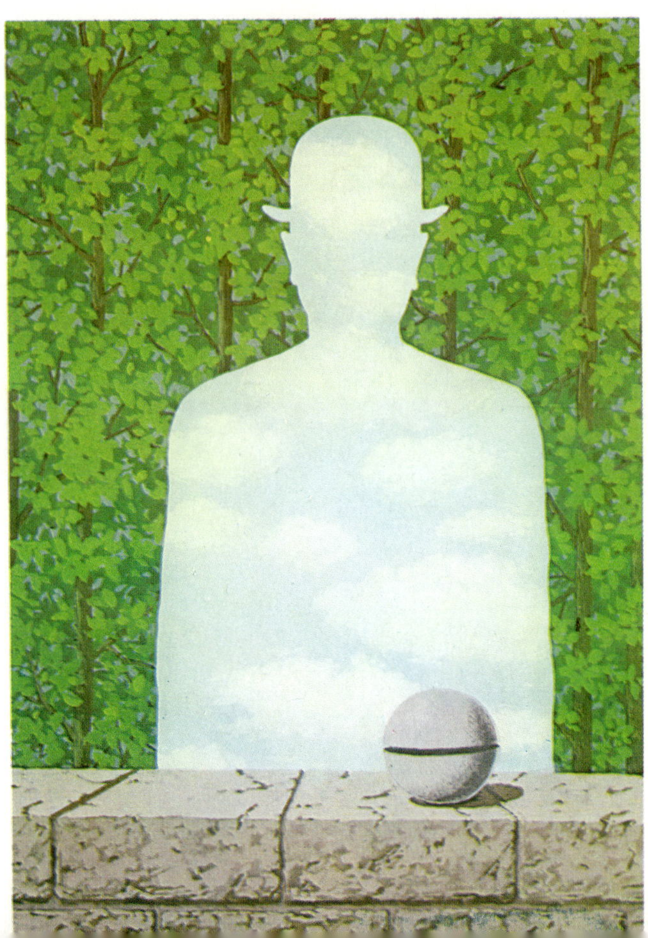

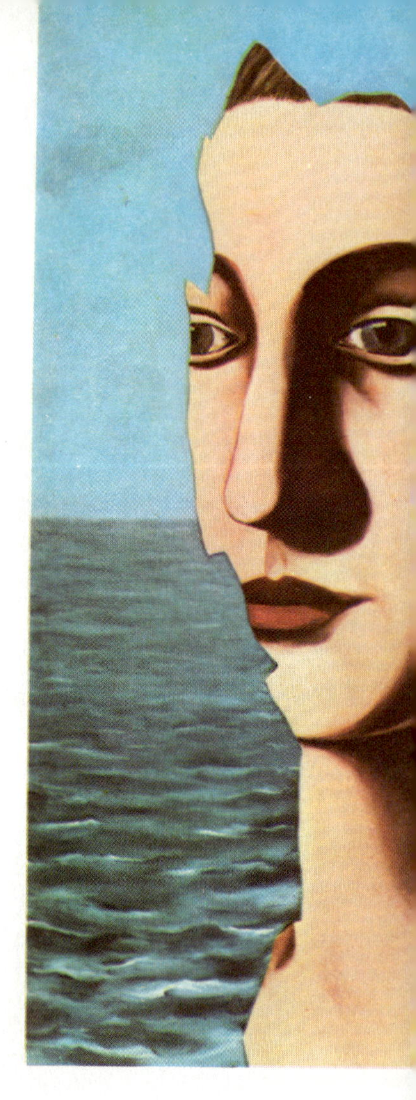

31
The deep secret
1928

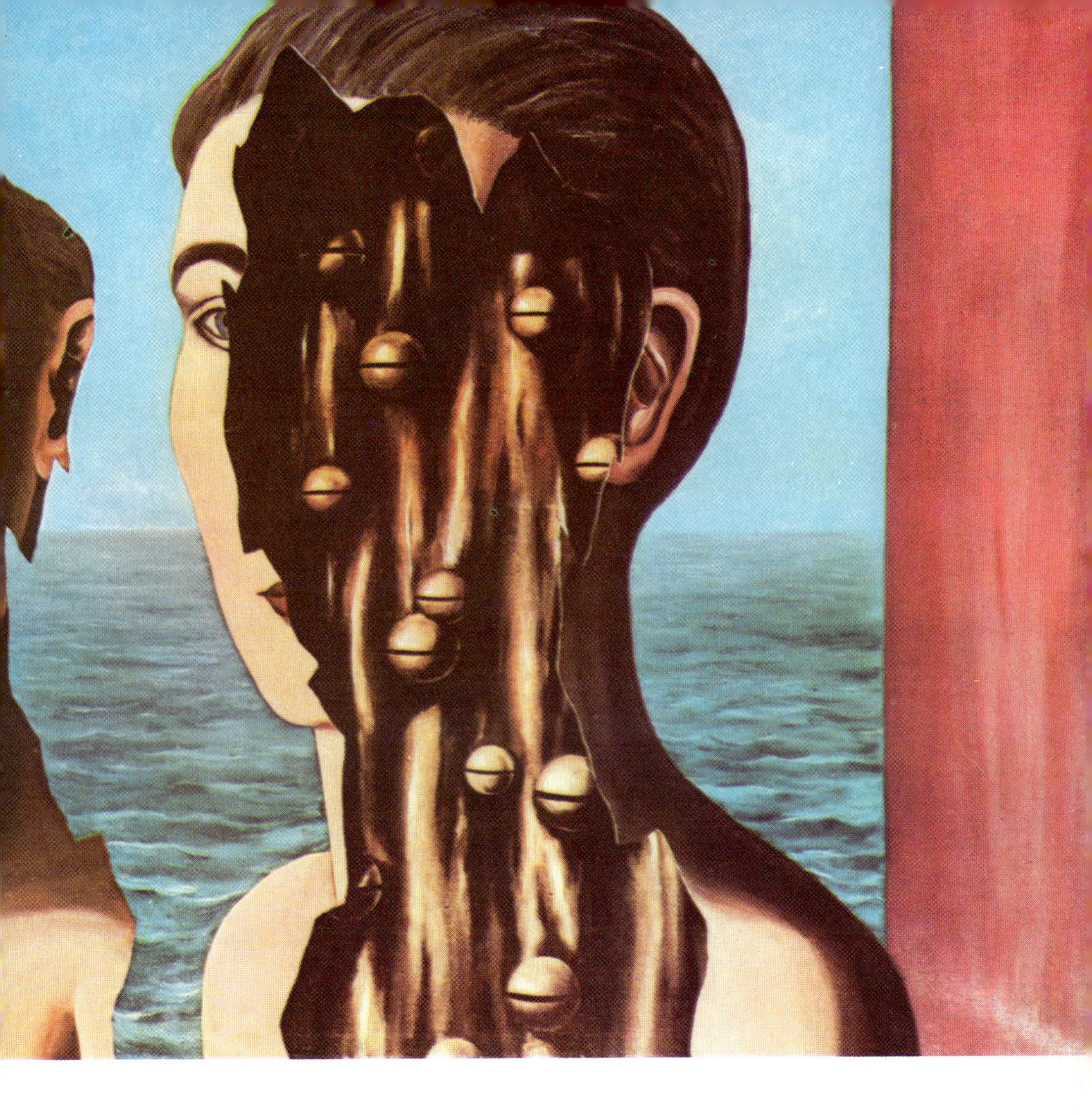

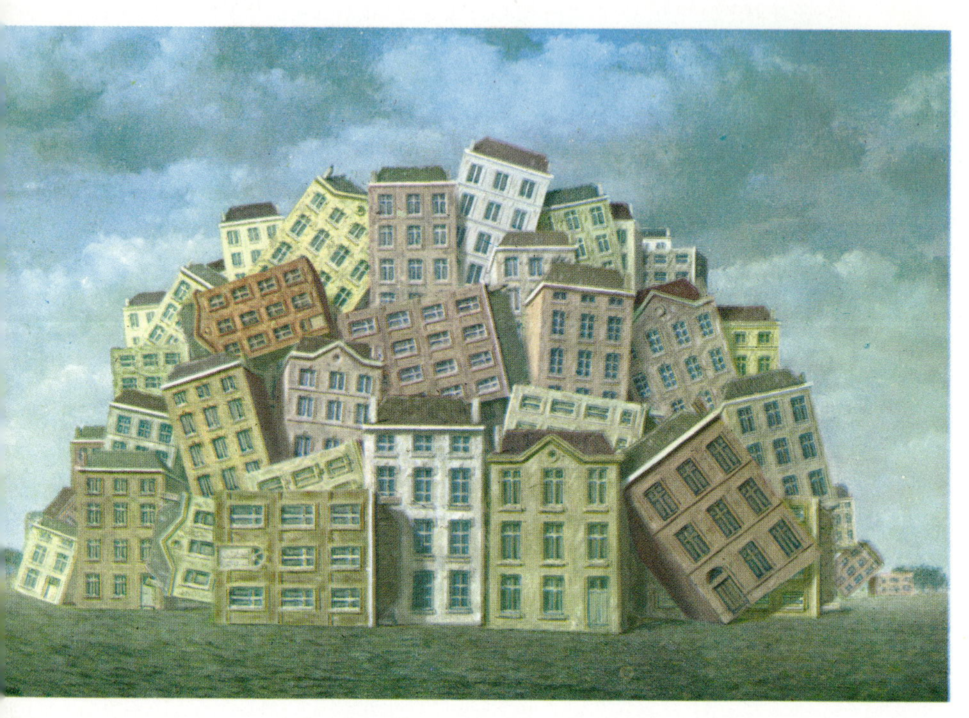

32
The chest
1960

33
Mental glance

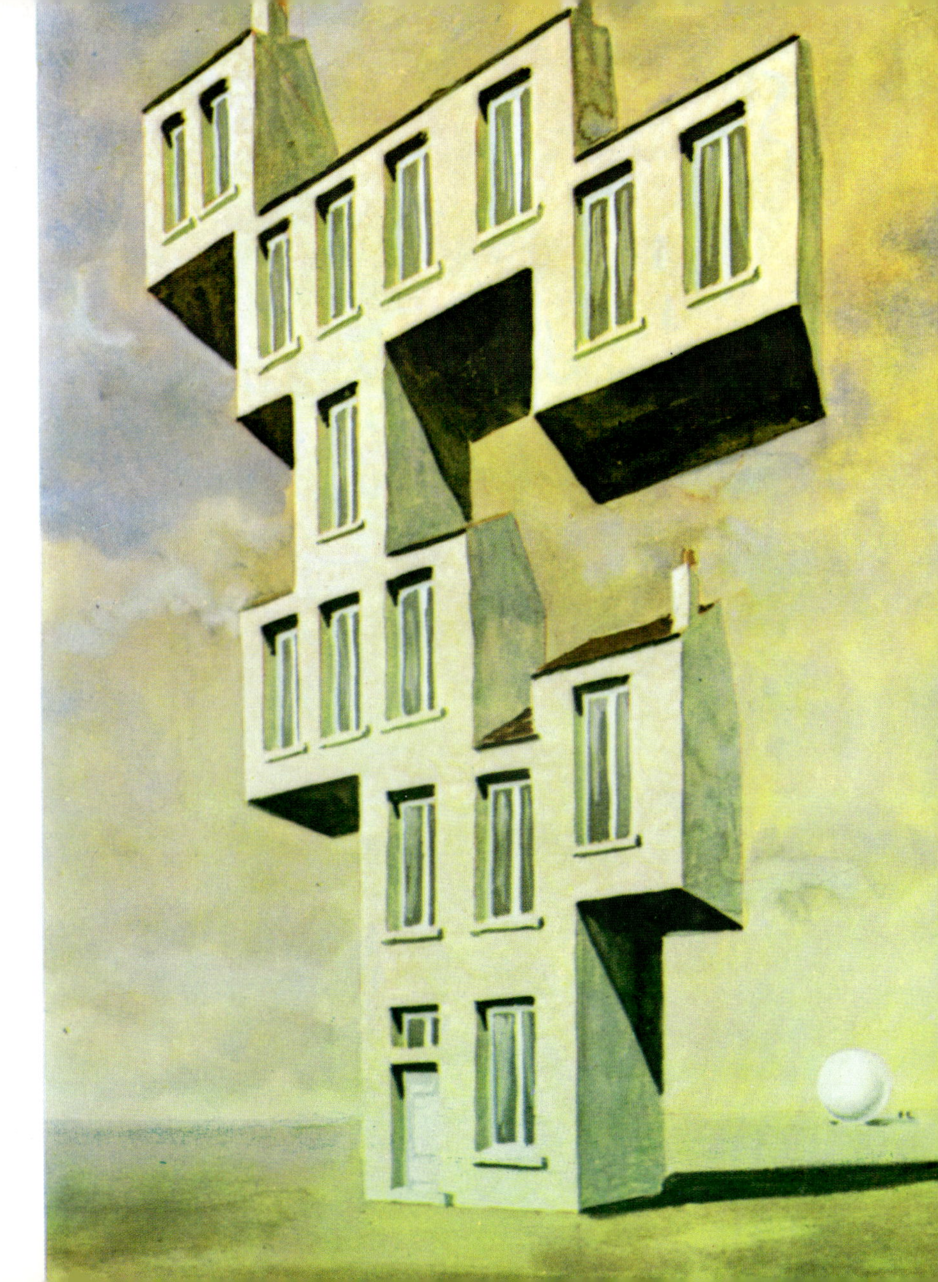

34
The use of words
1935

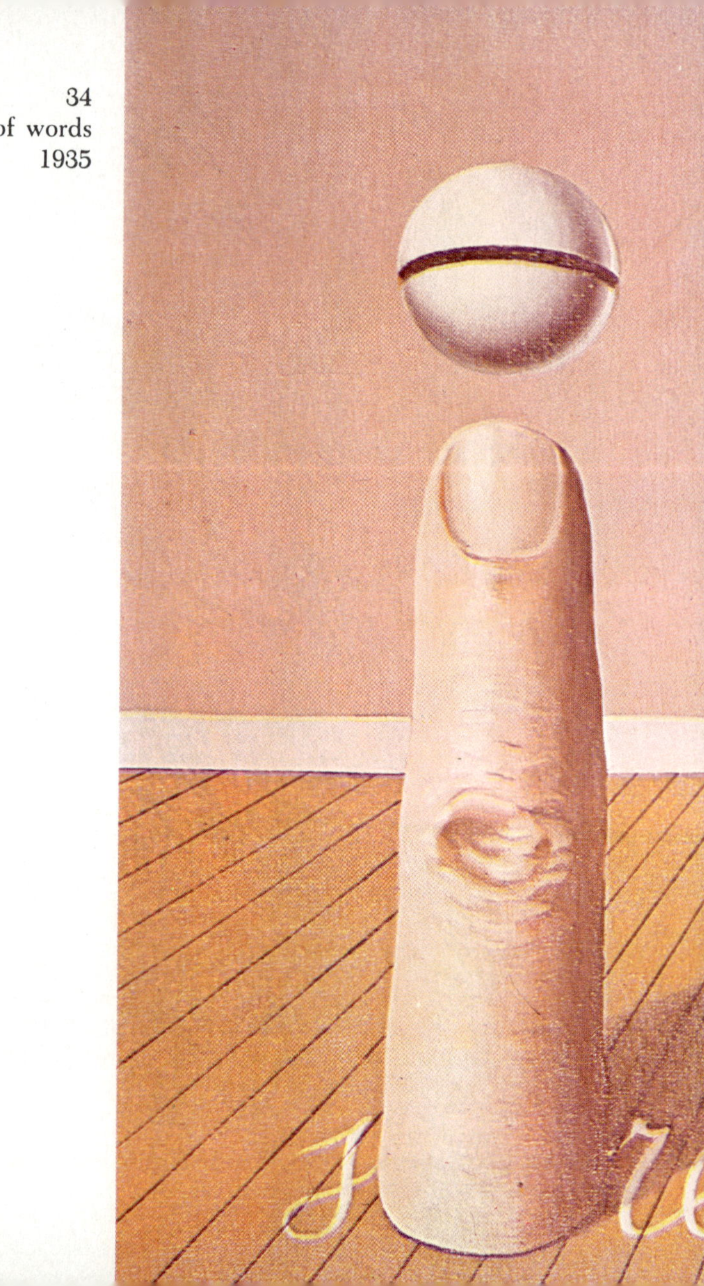

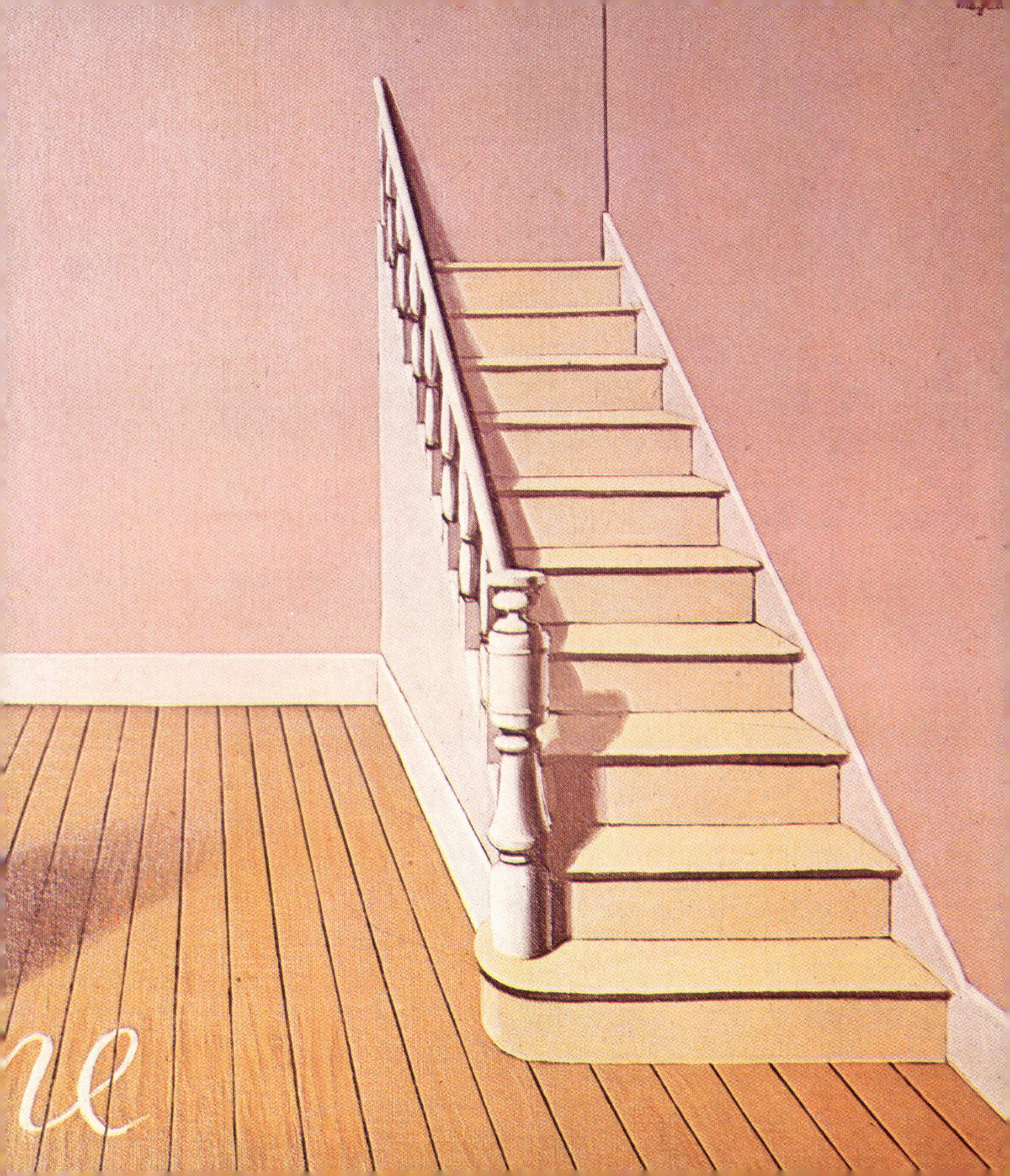

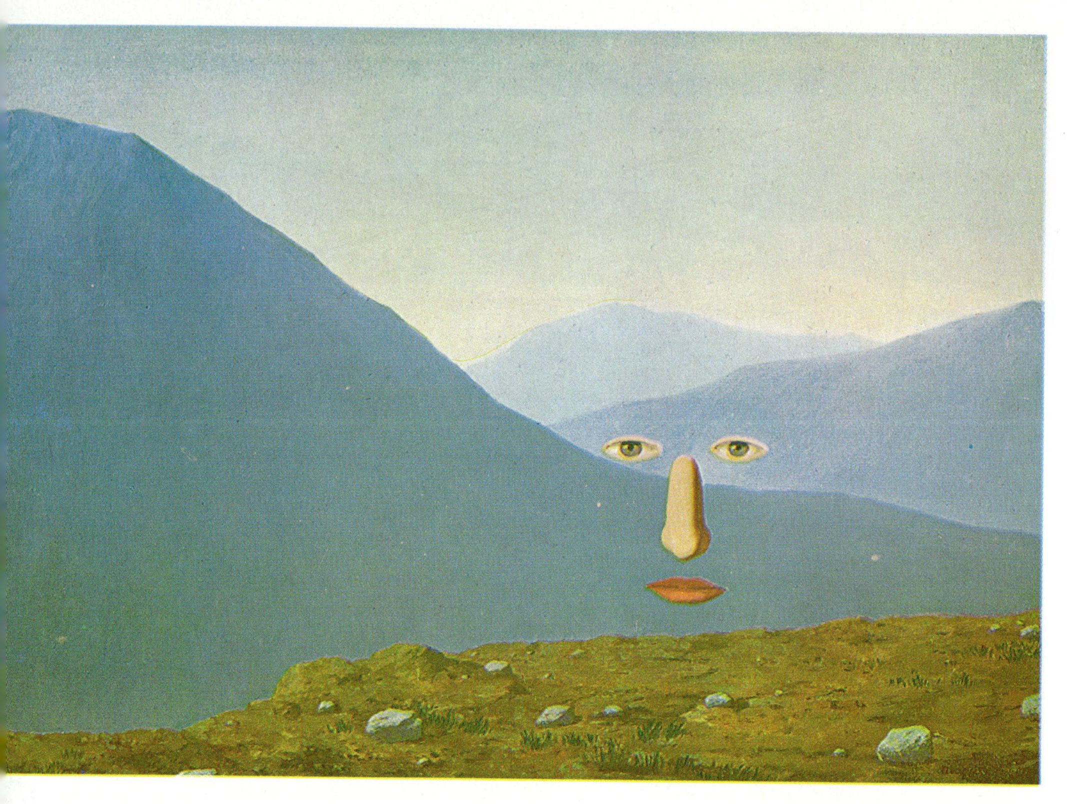

35
Everyday
1966

36
The landscape of Baucis
1966

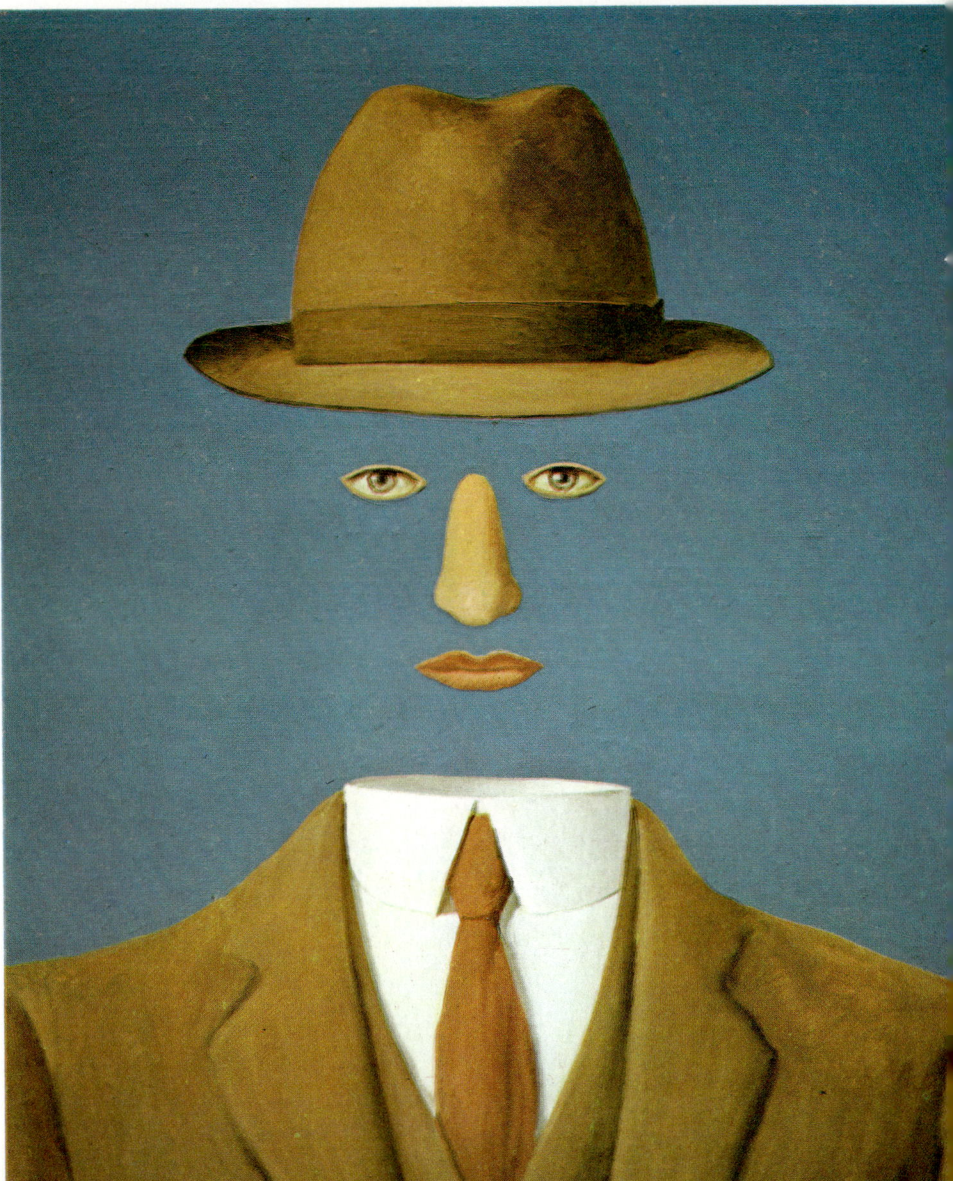

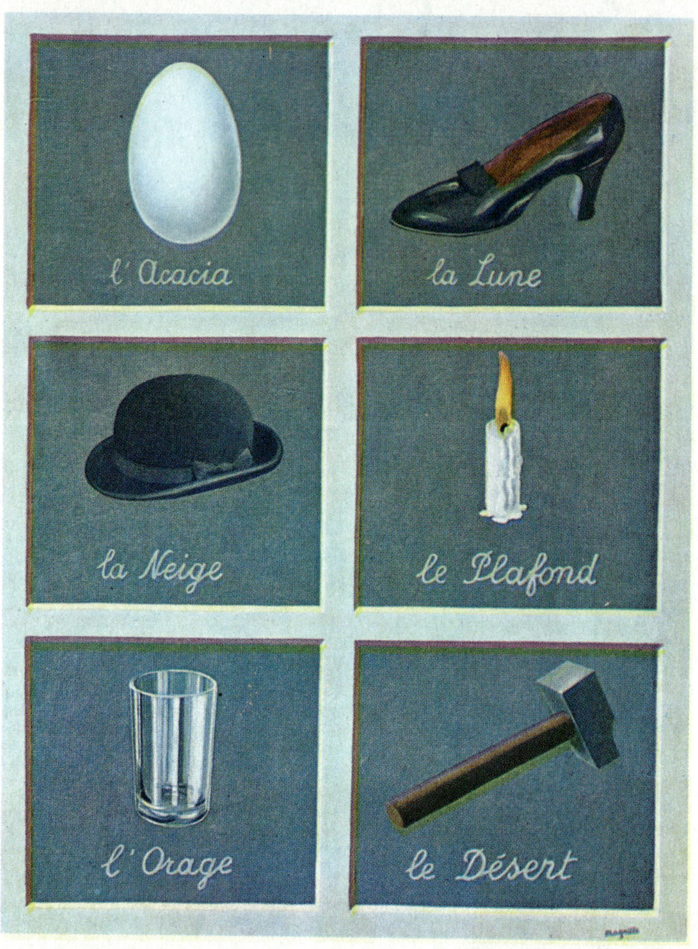

37
The key to dreams
1930

38
Hegel's holiday
1958

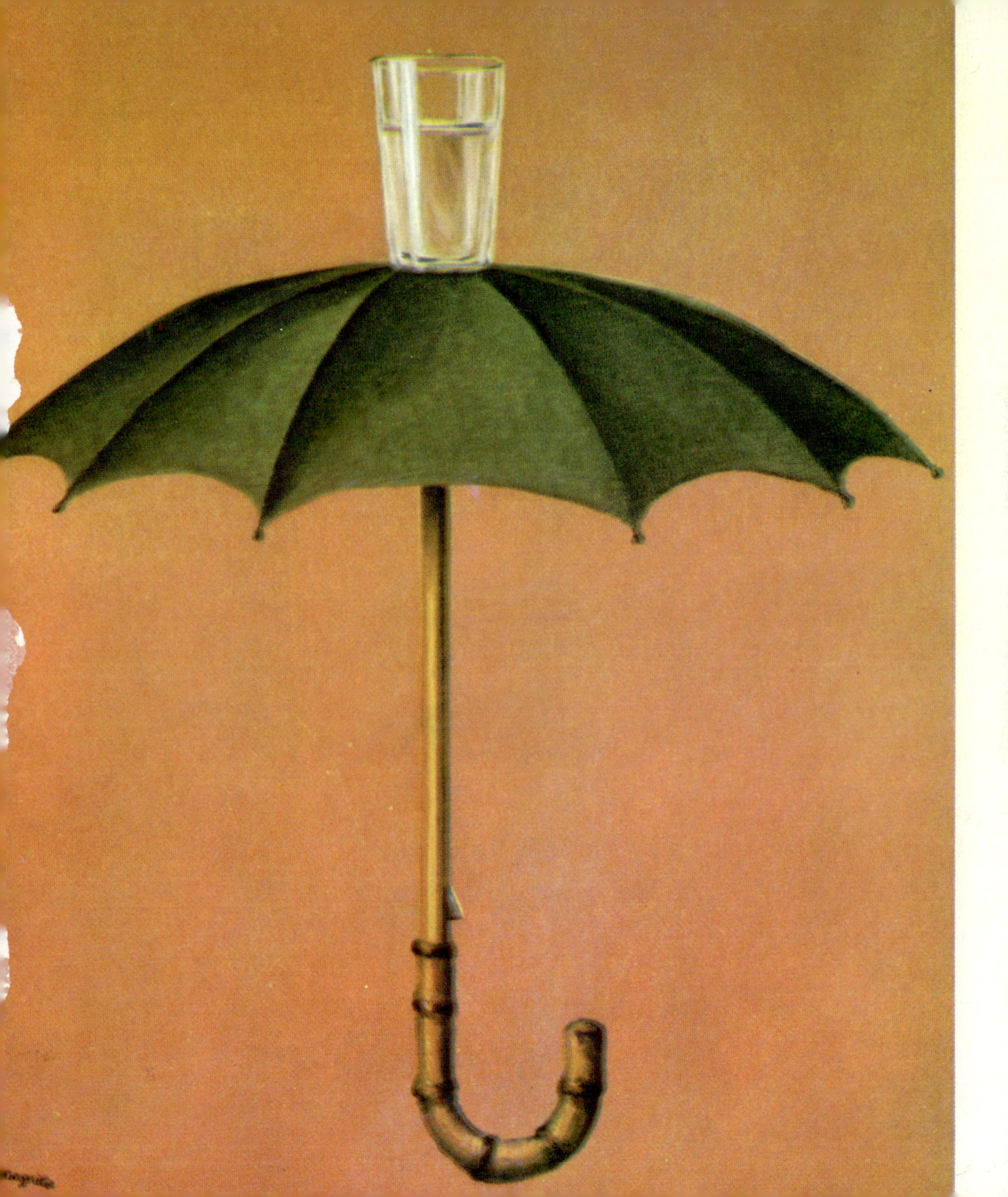

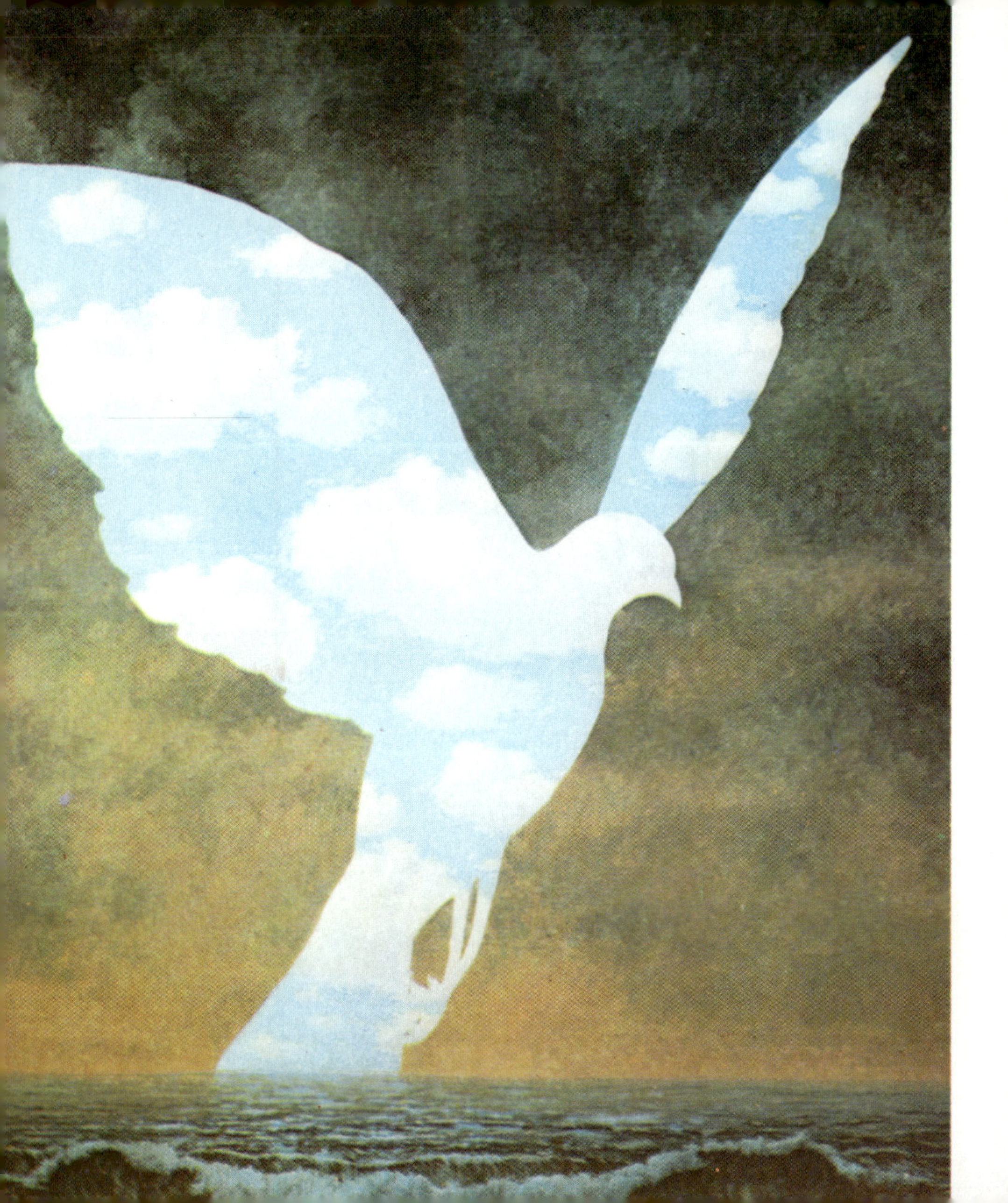

39
The large family
1947

40
The victory
1939

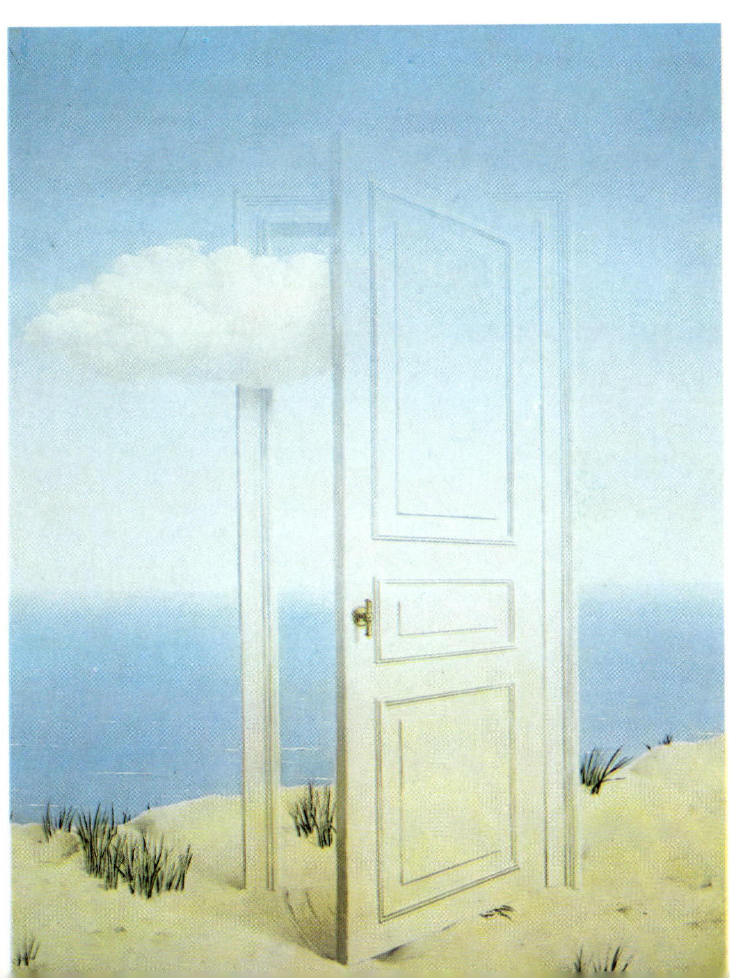

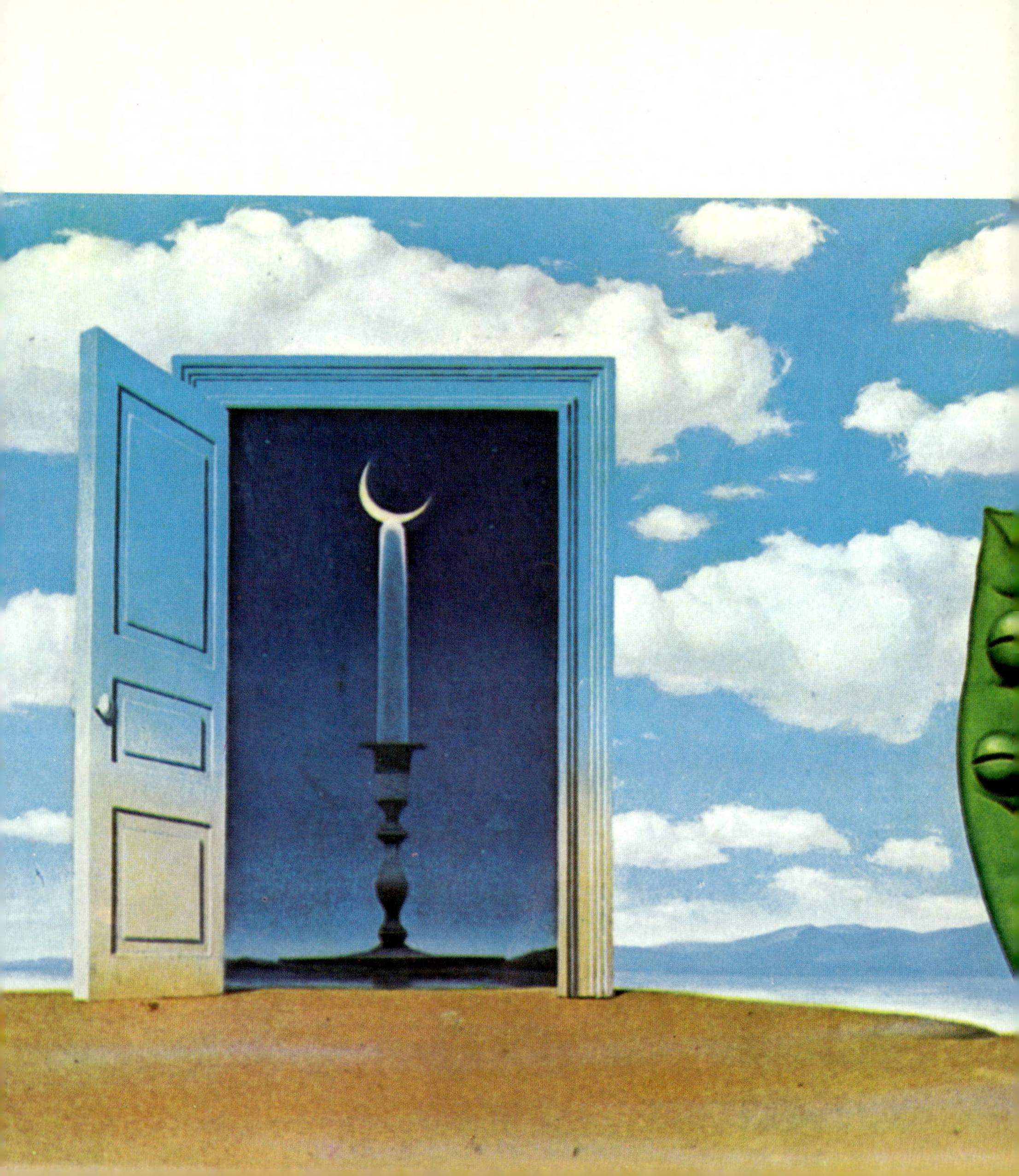

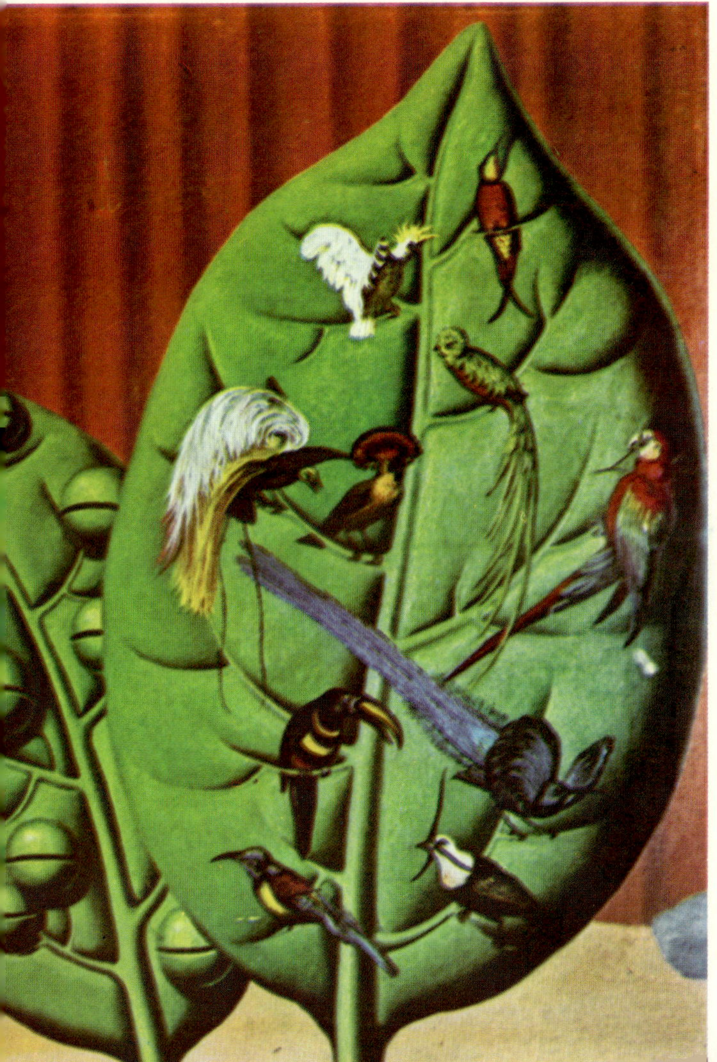

41
The enchanted domain
1952

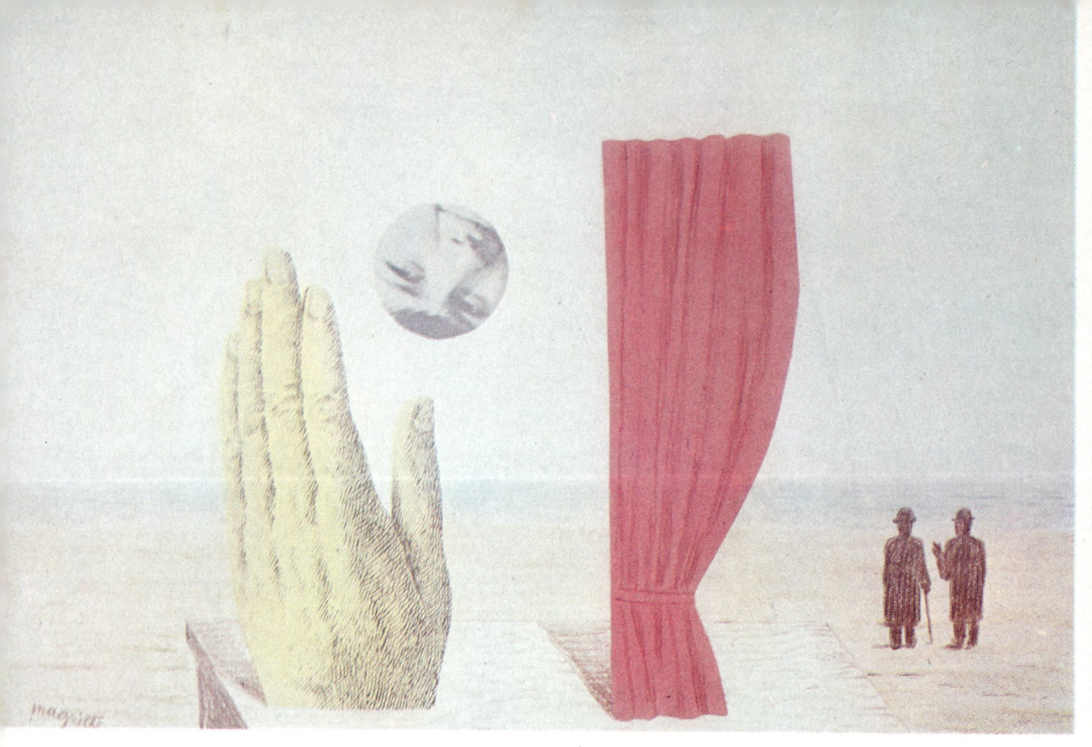

42
Untitled

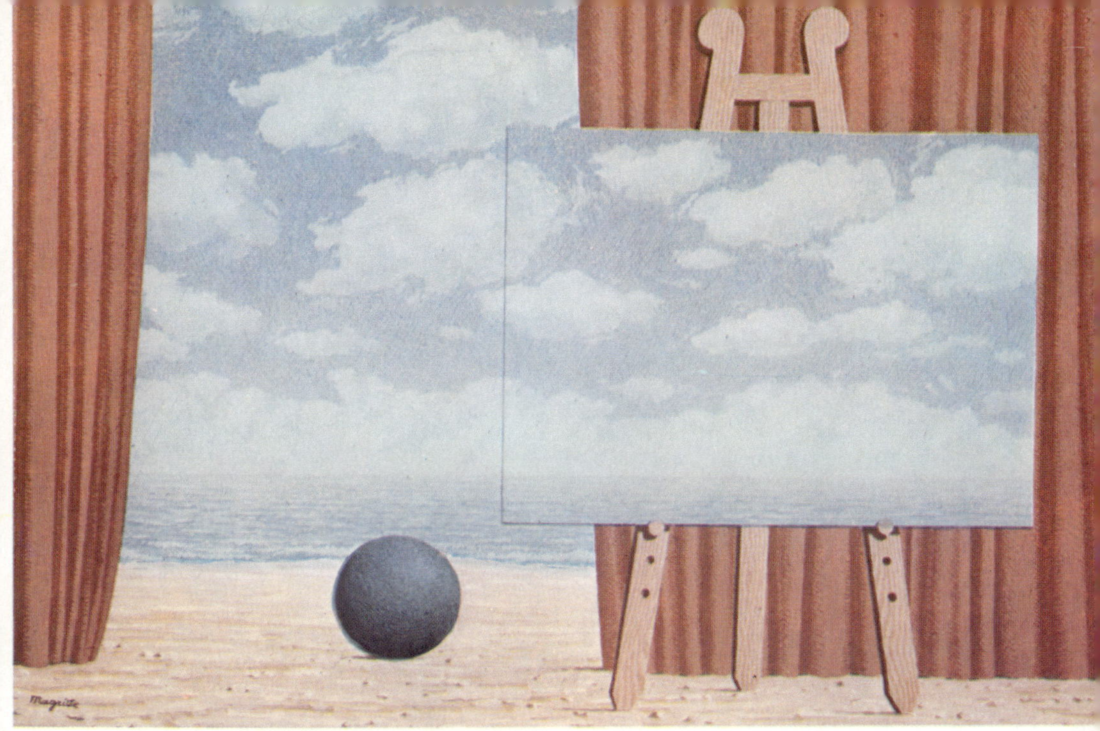

43
The beautiful captive

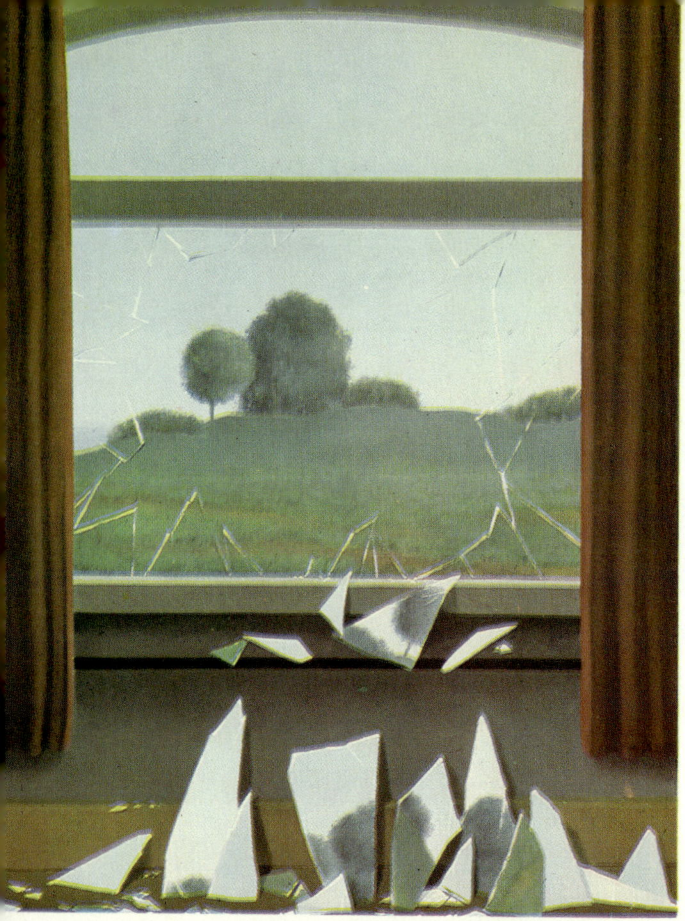

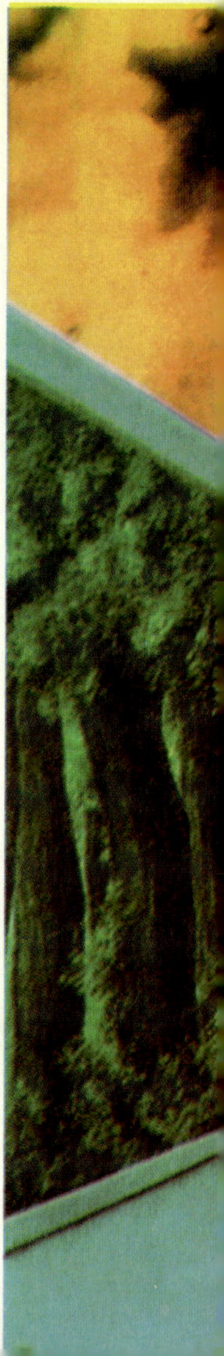

44
The key to the fields
1933

45
At the threshold of liberty
1929

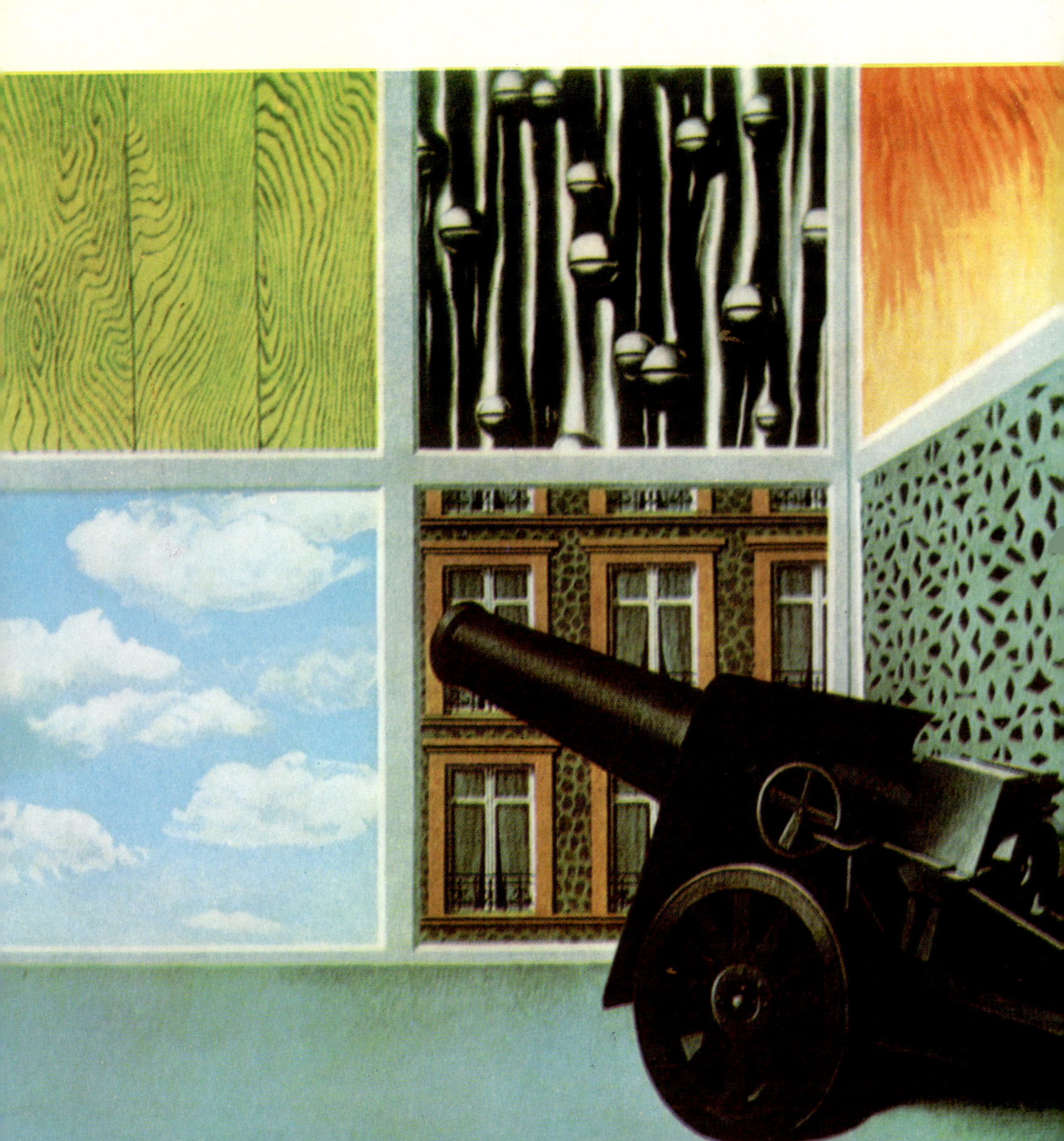

46
The break of day
1967

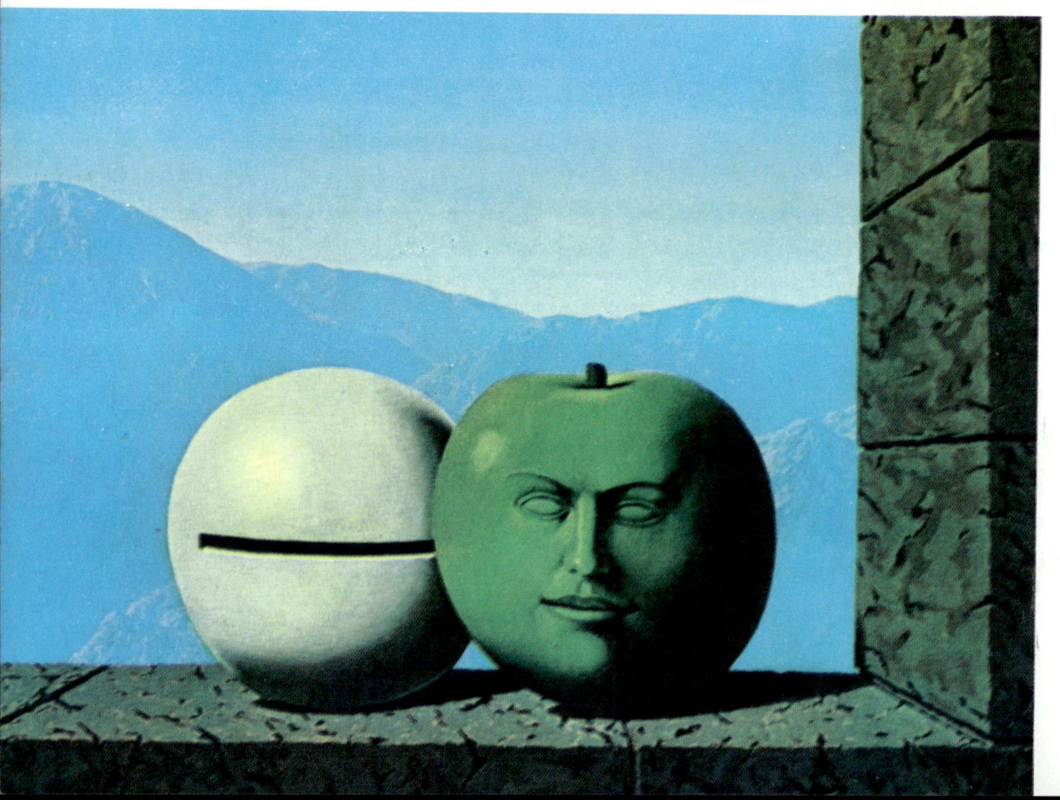

47
Perpetual motion
1934

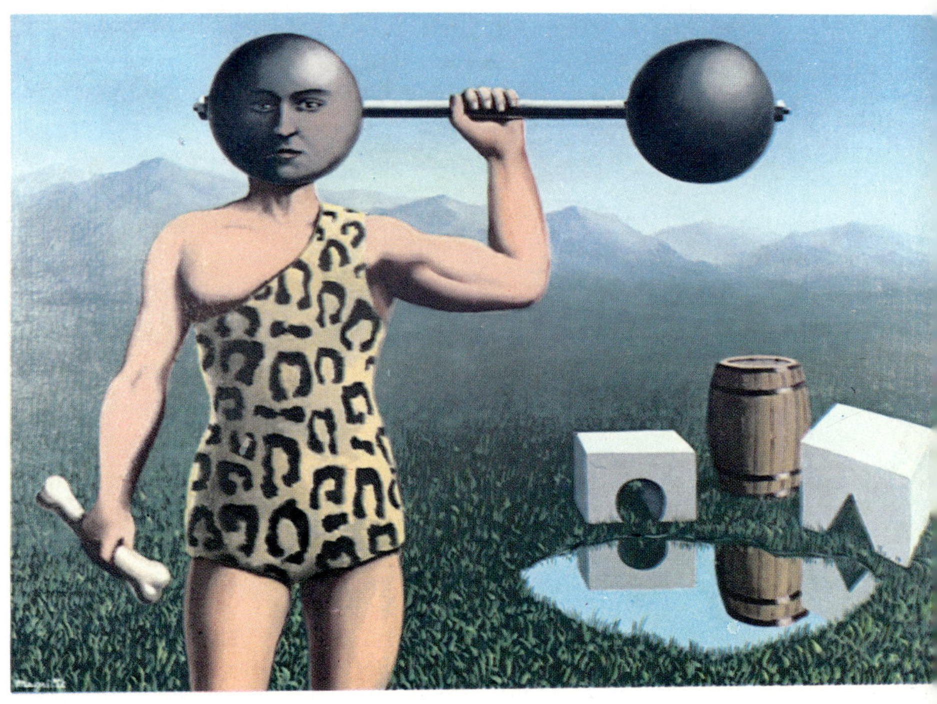

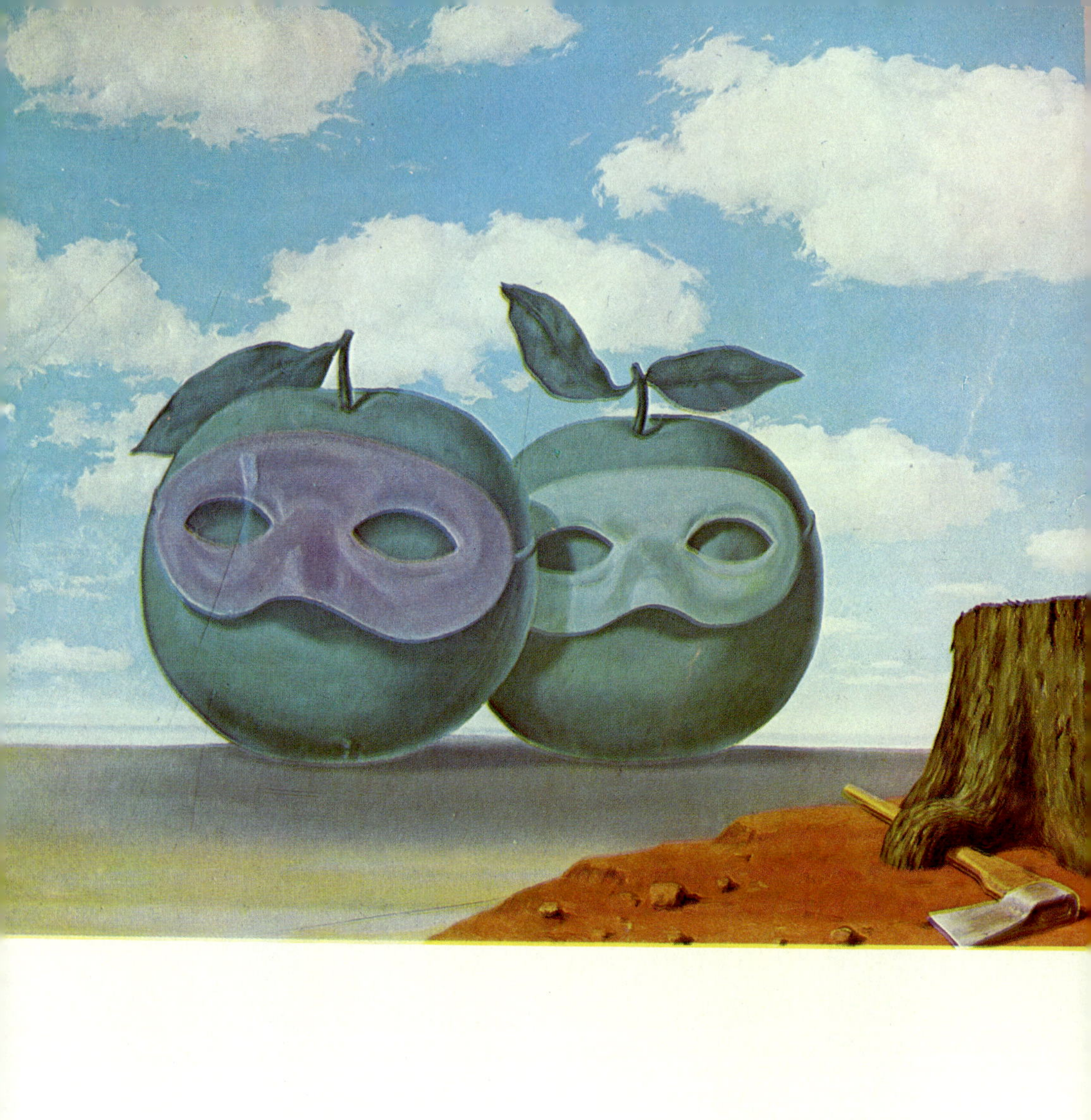

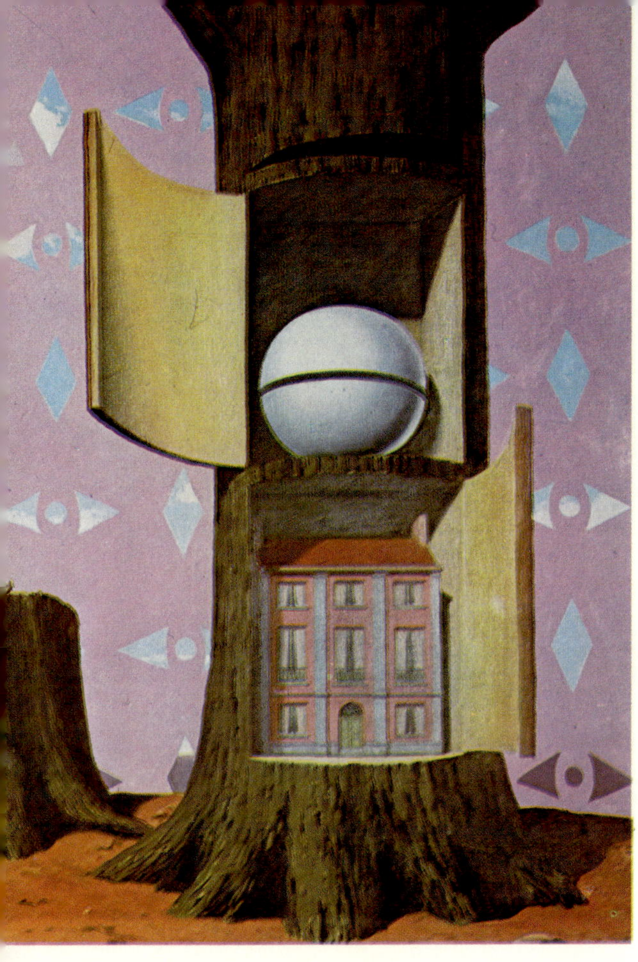

48
The enchanted domain
1950

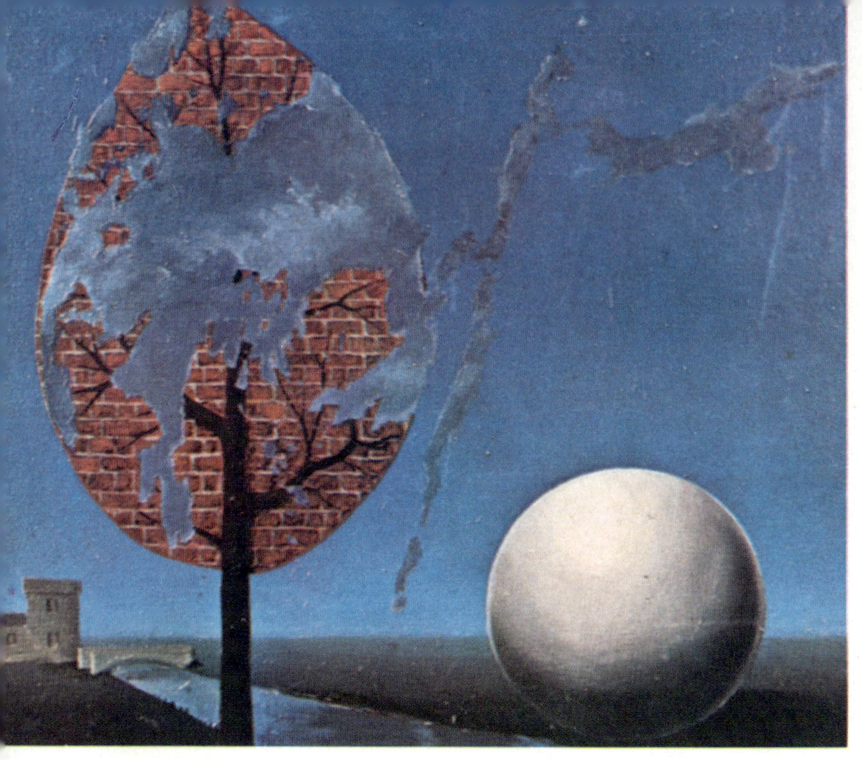

49
Passionflower
1936

50
The voice of the winds
1932

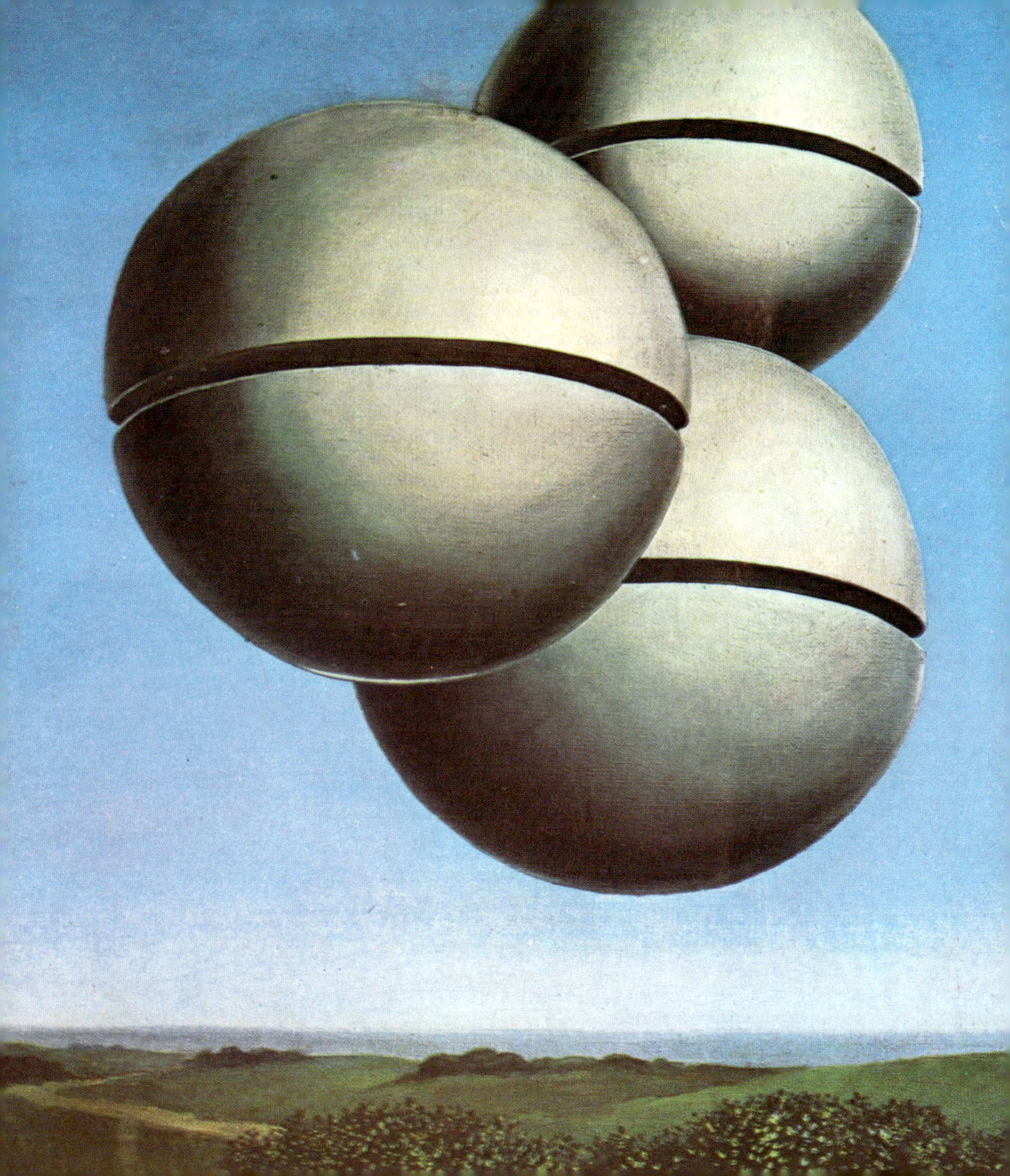

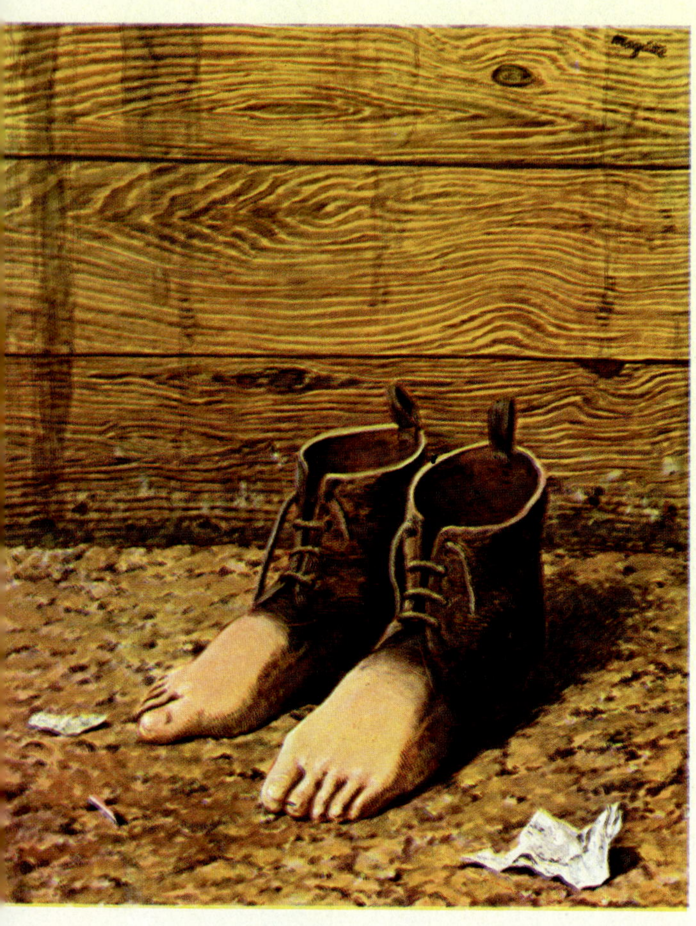

51
The rose model
1947

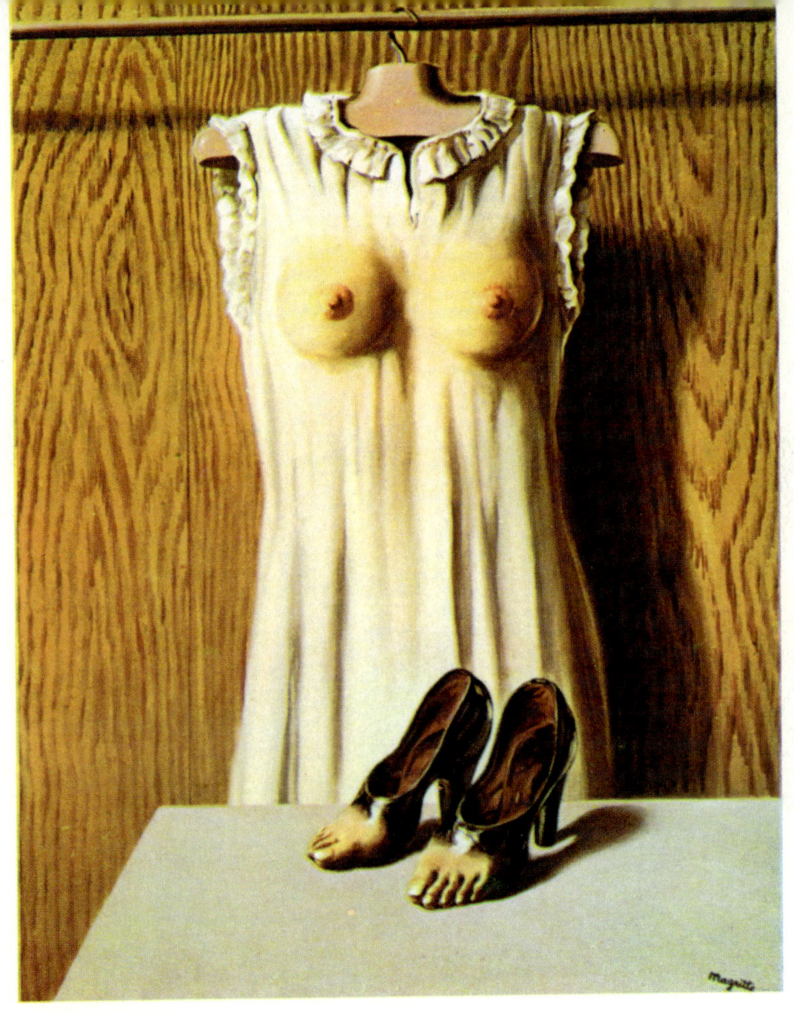

52
Philosophy in the bedroom
1947

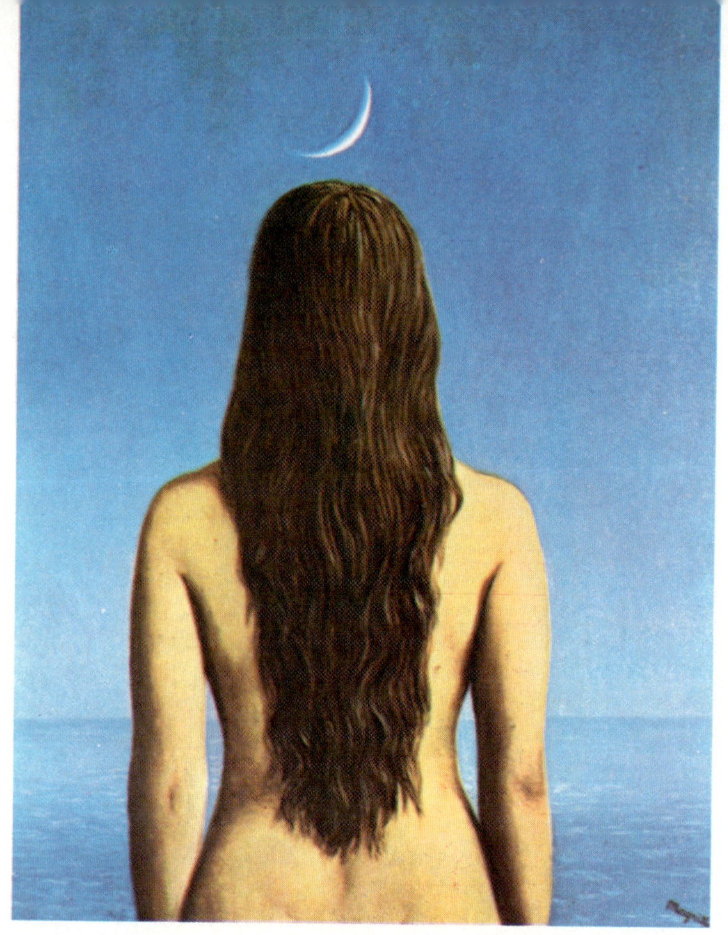

53
The dress of night
1954

54
The rape
1934

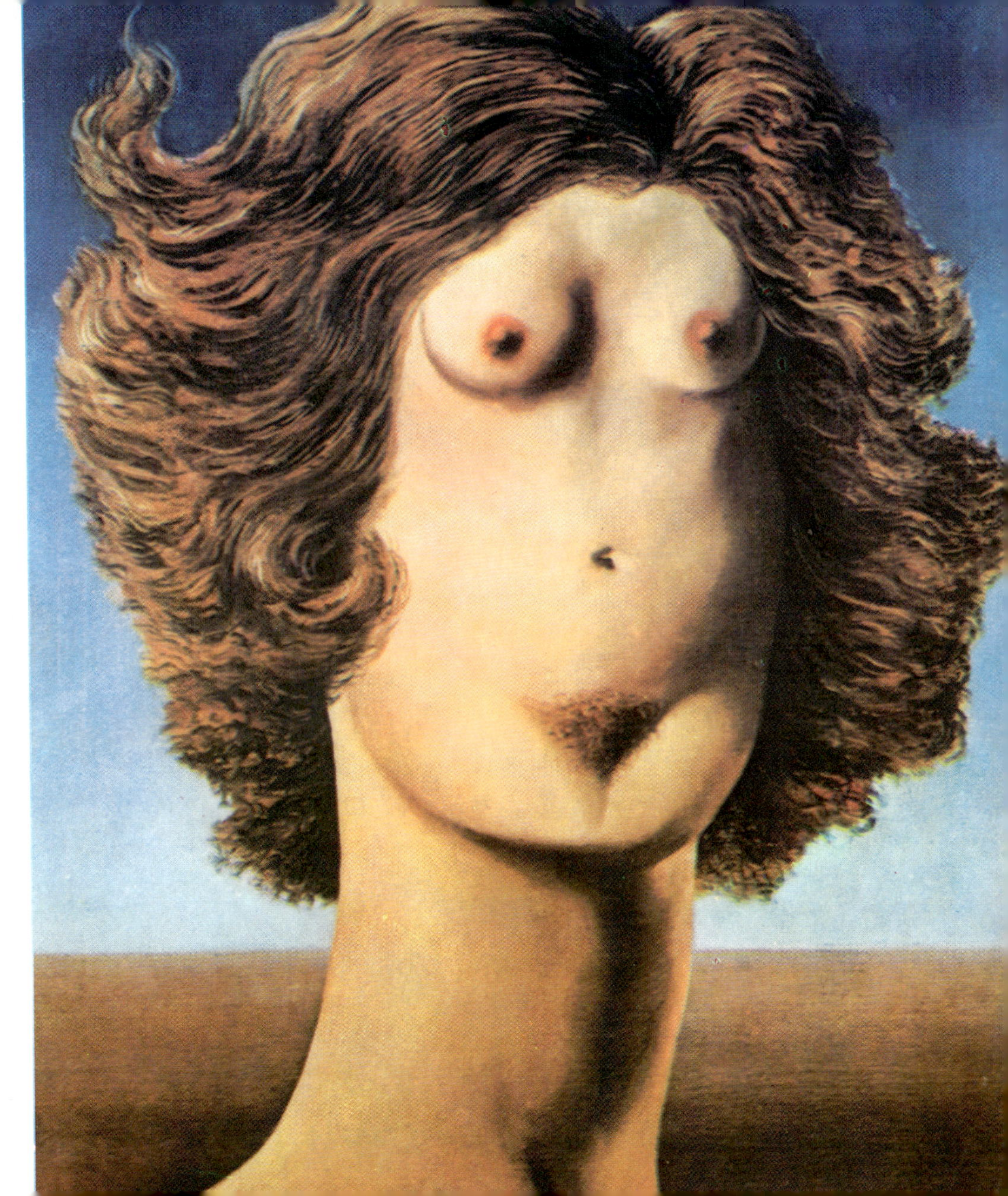

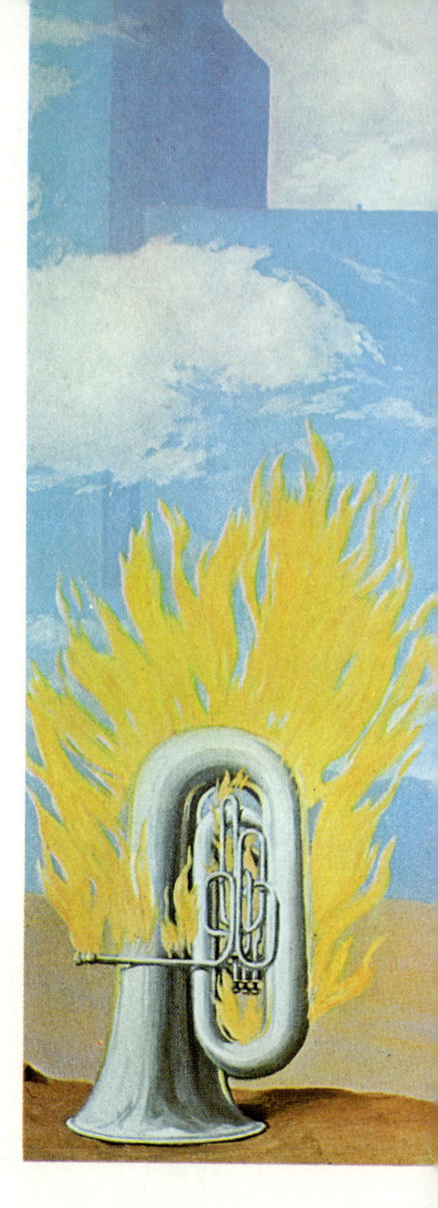

55
The enchanted domain
1952

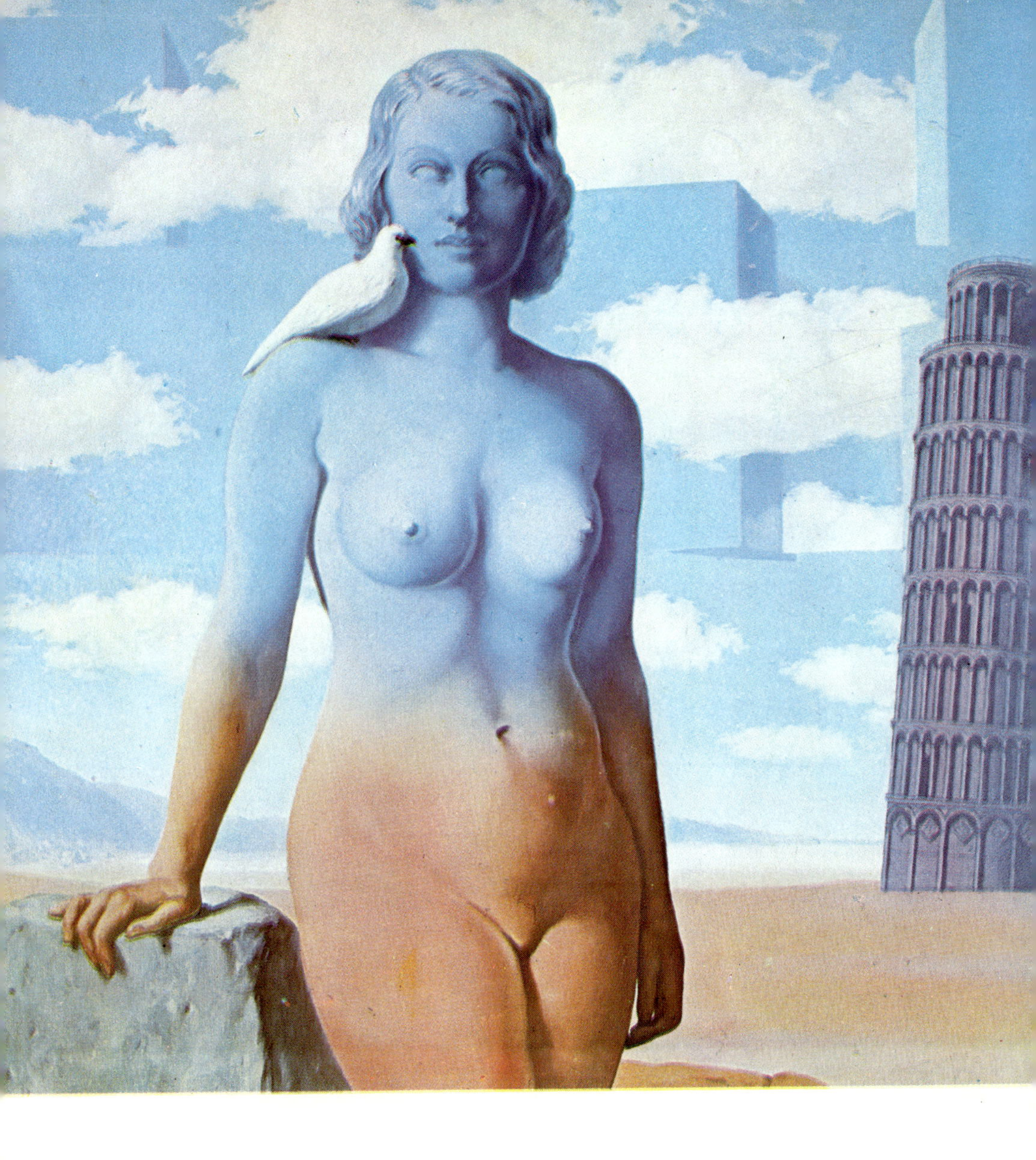

56
Summer walks
1938

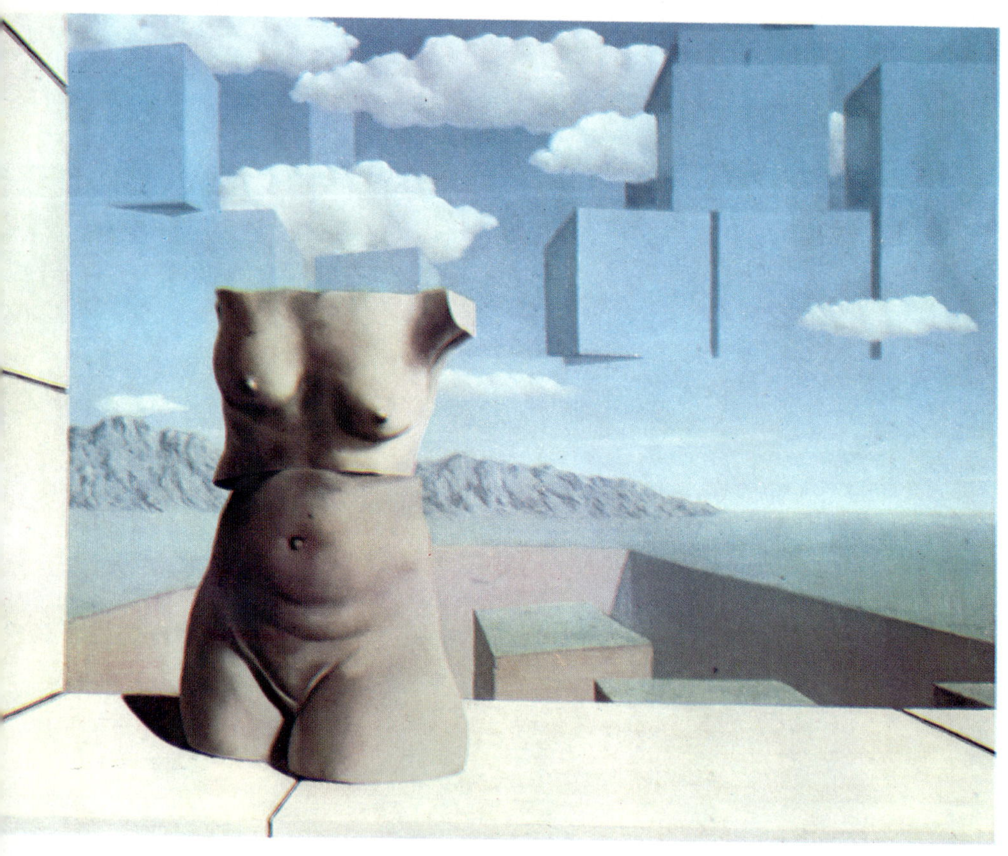

57
The enchanted domain (detail)
1952

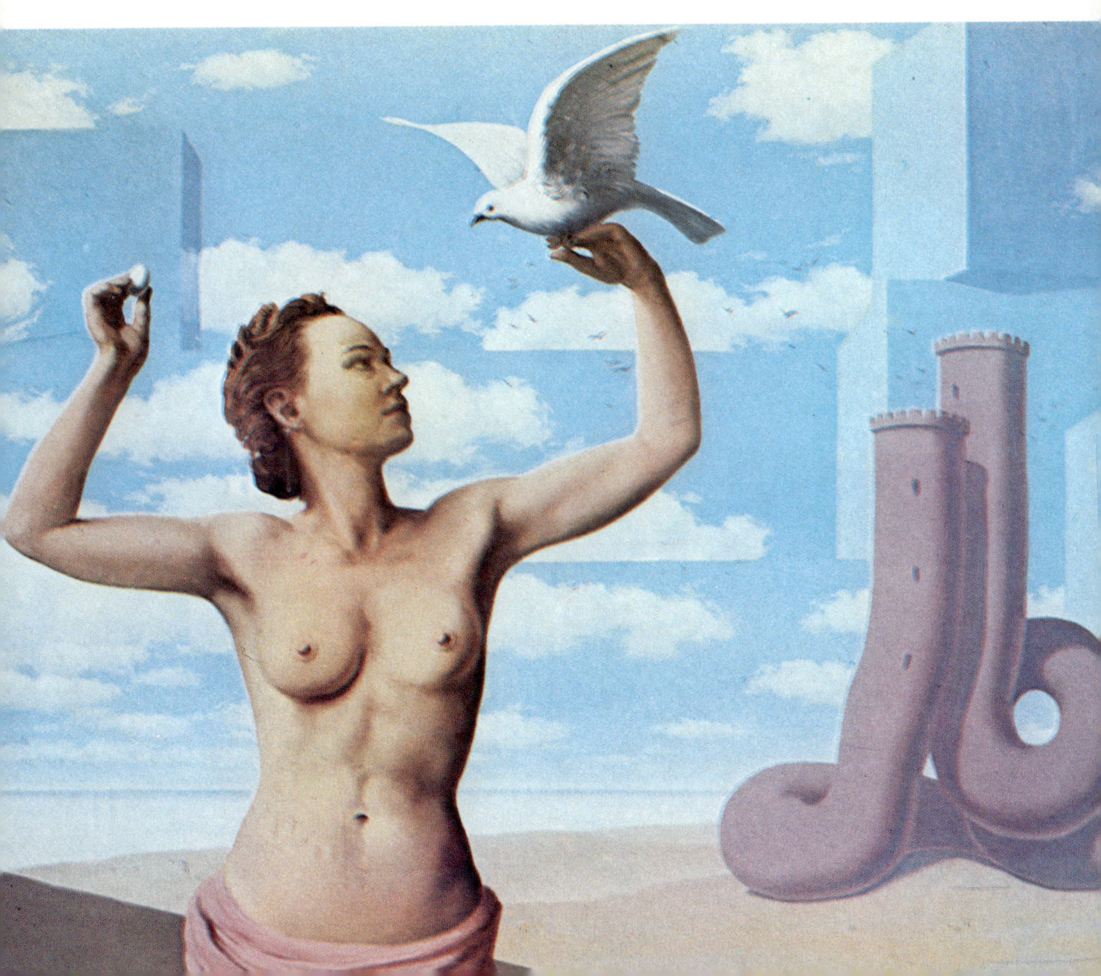

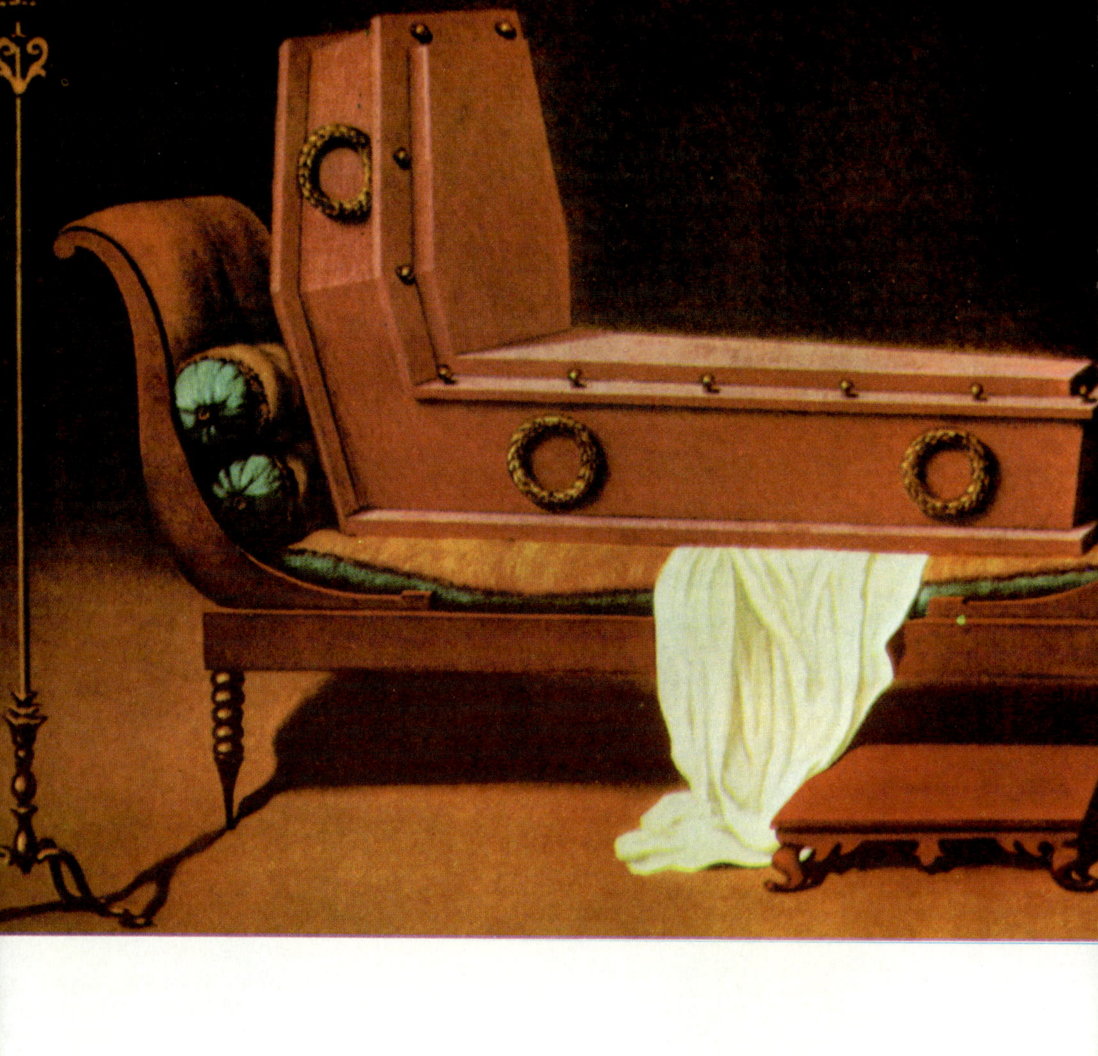

58
Madame Recamier by David
1950

59
Manet's balcony
1950

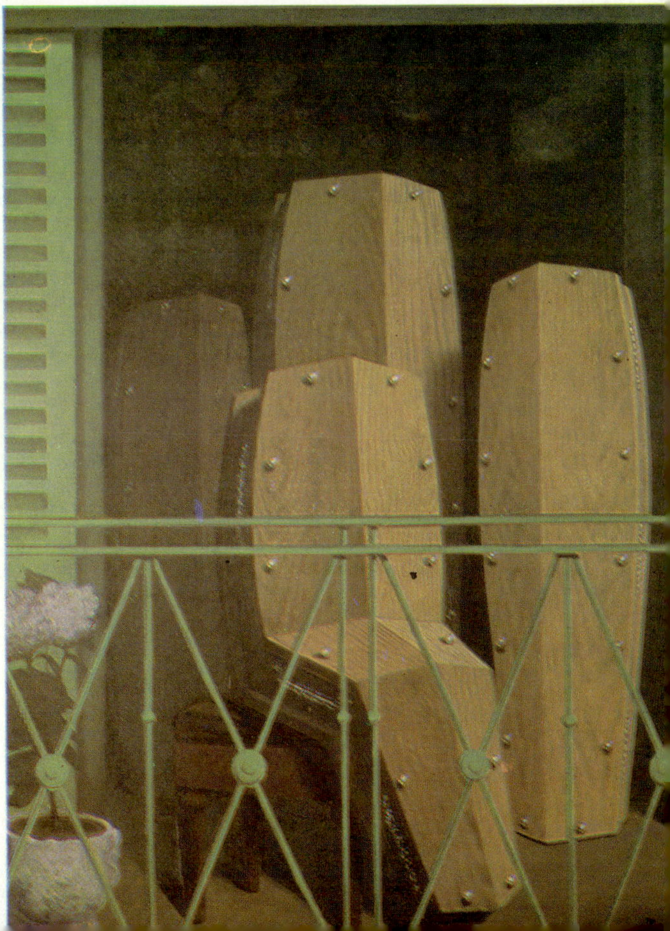

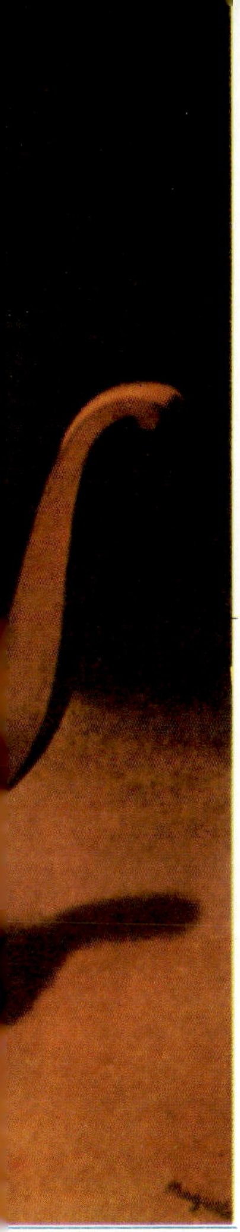

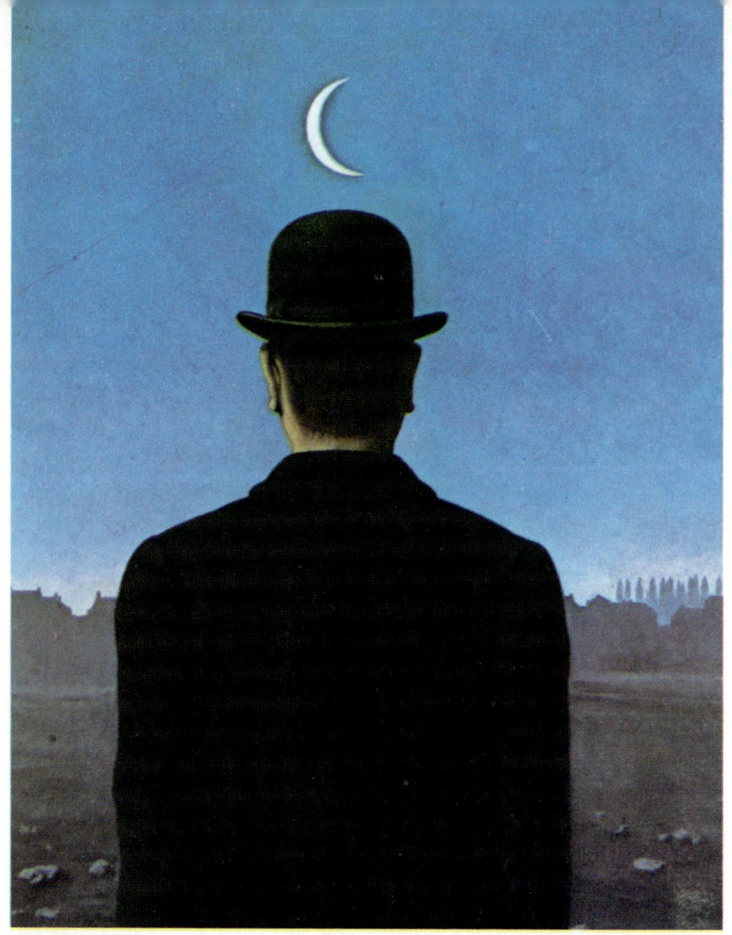

60
The schoolmaster
1954

61
Order's friend
1964

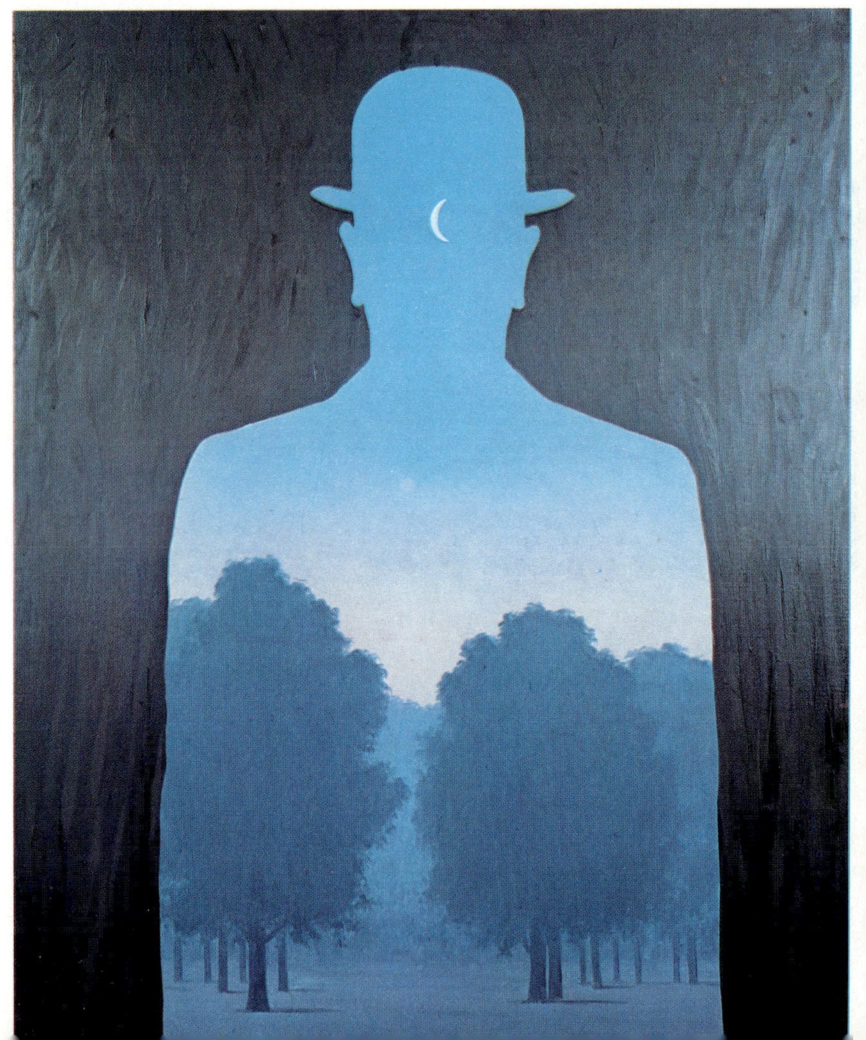

62
The month of the harvest
1959

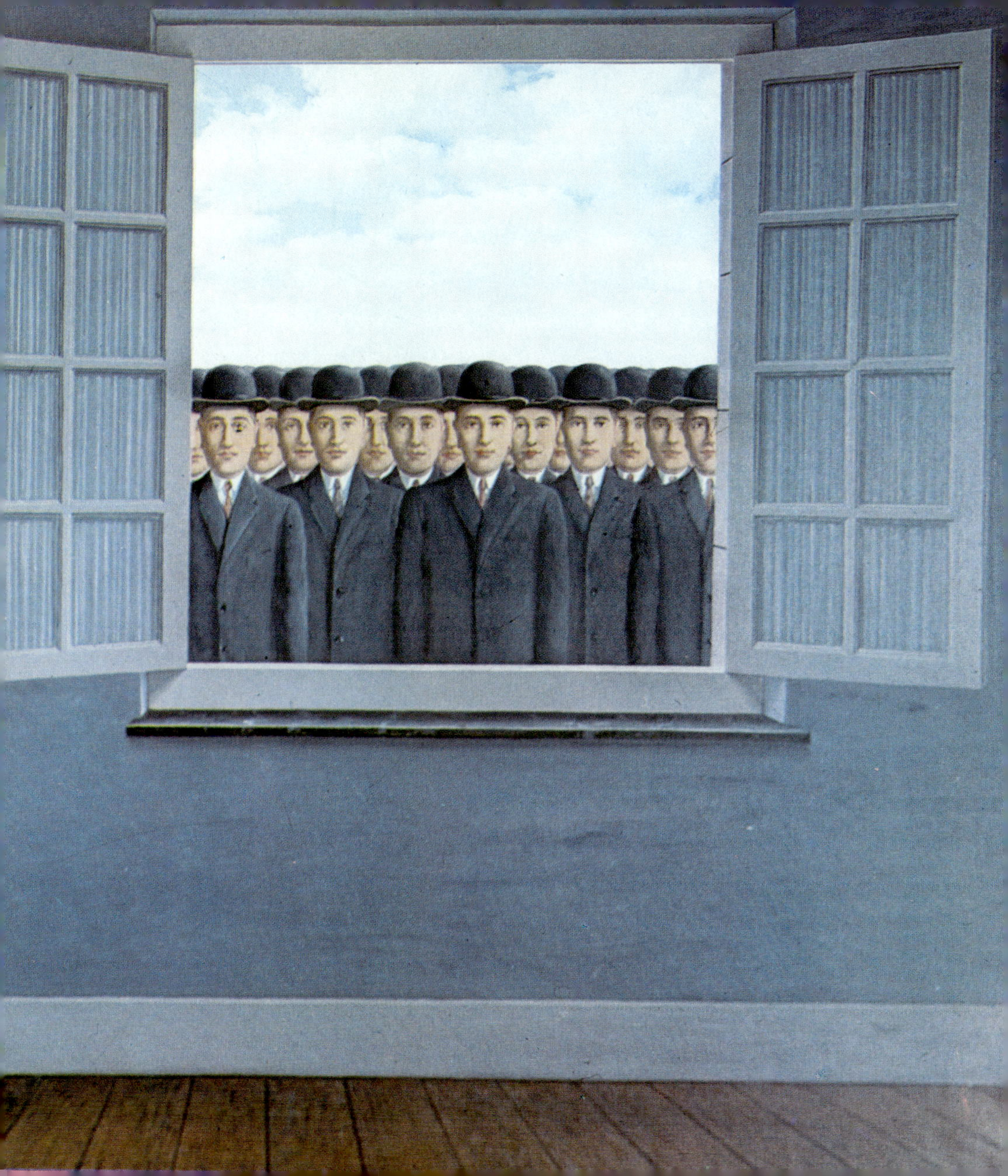

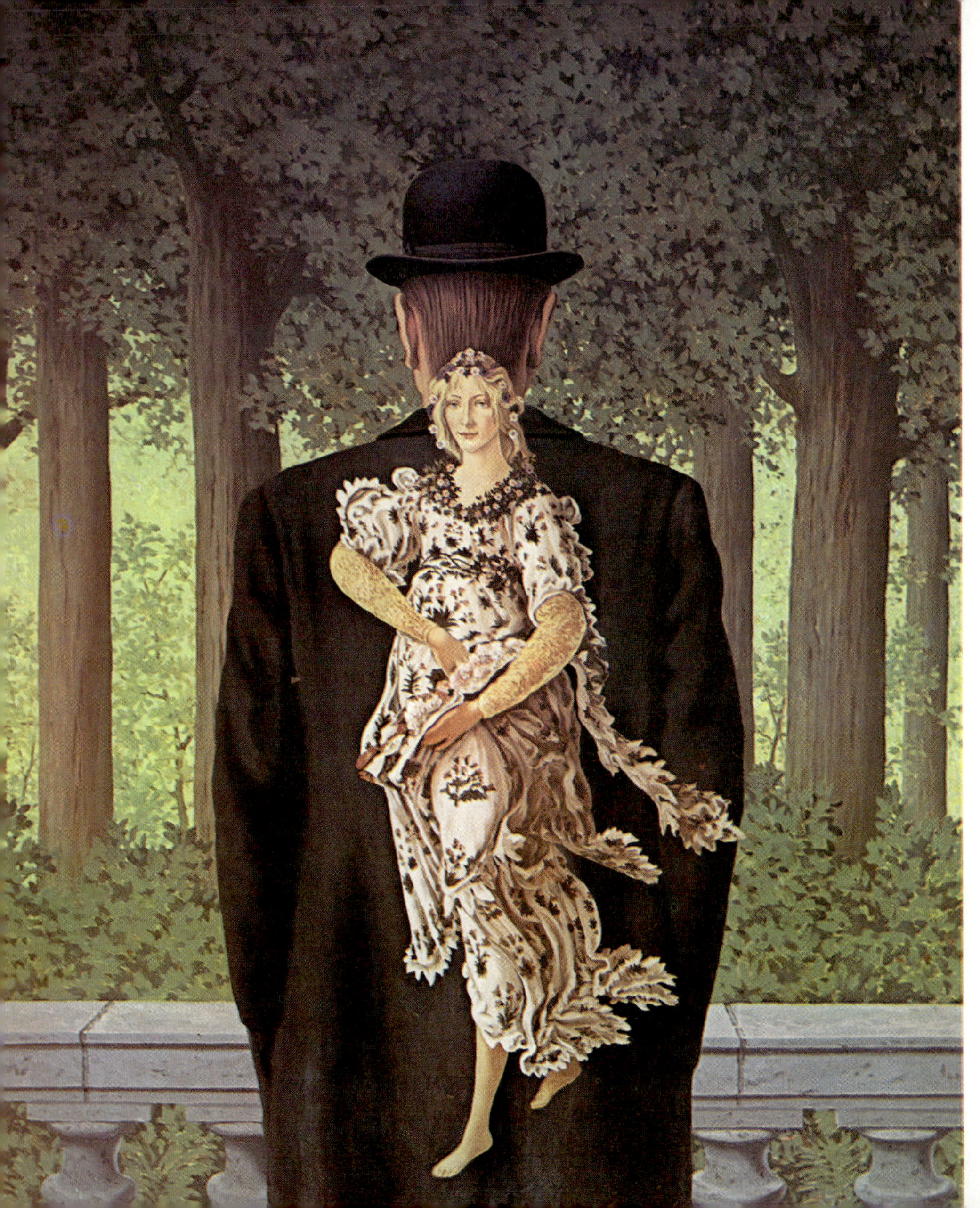

63
The ready-made bouquet (detail)
1956

64
Title Unknown

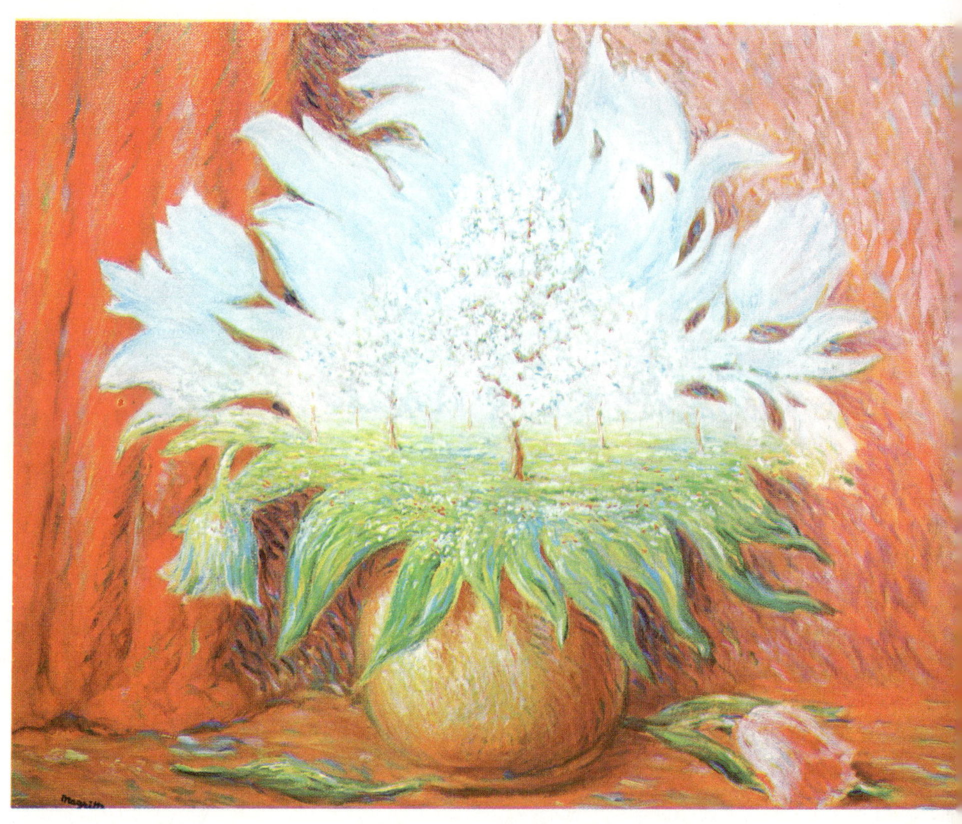

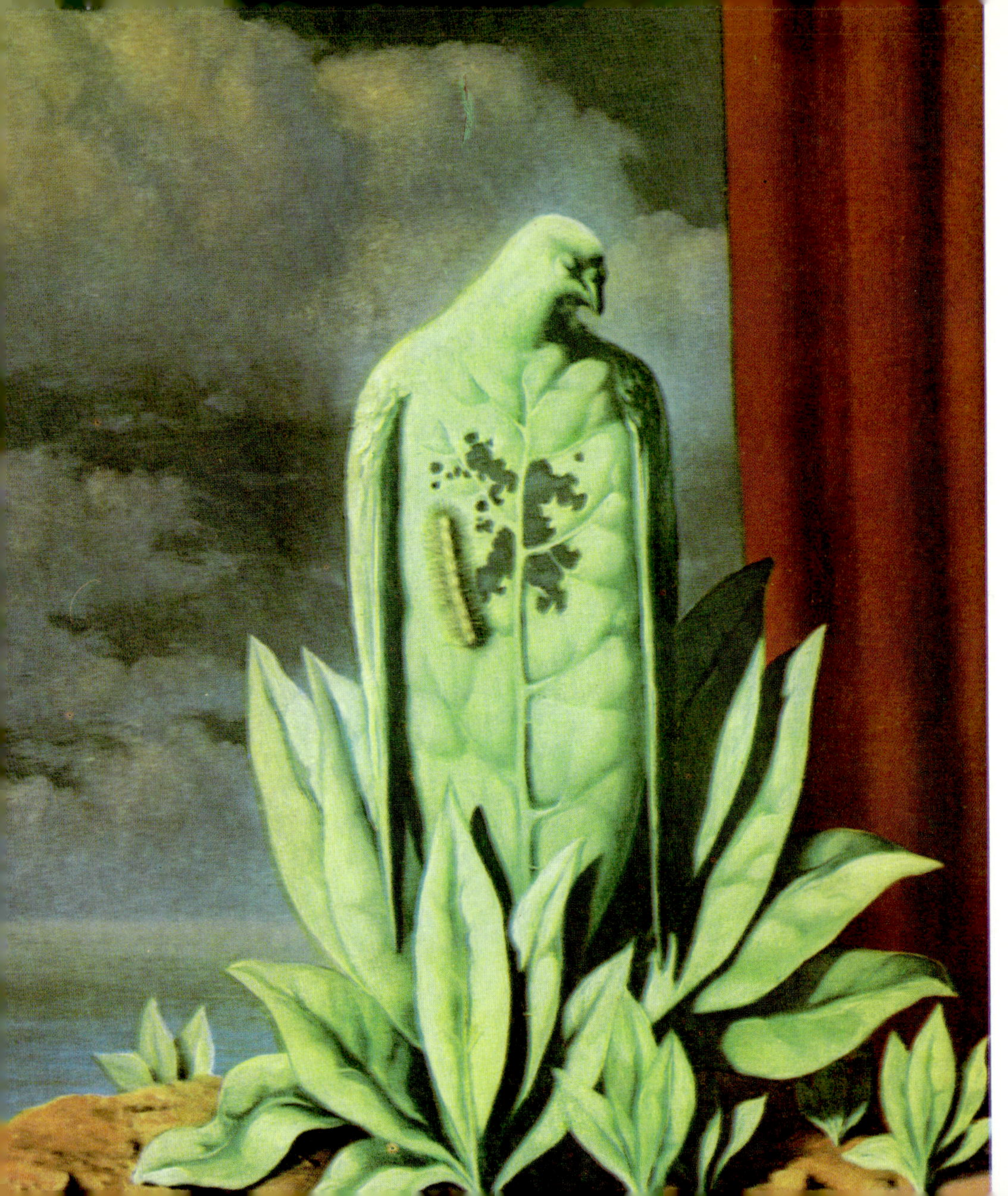

65 The flavor of tears 1948

66 The enchanted domain (detail) 1952

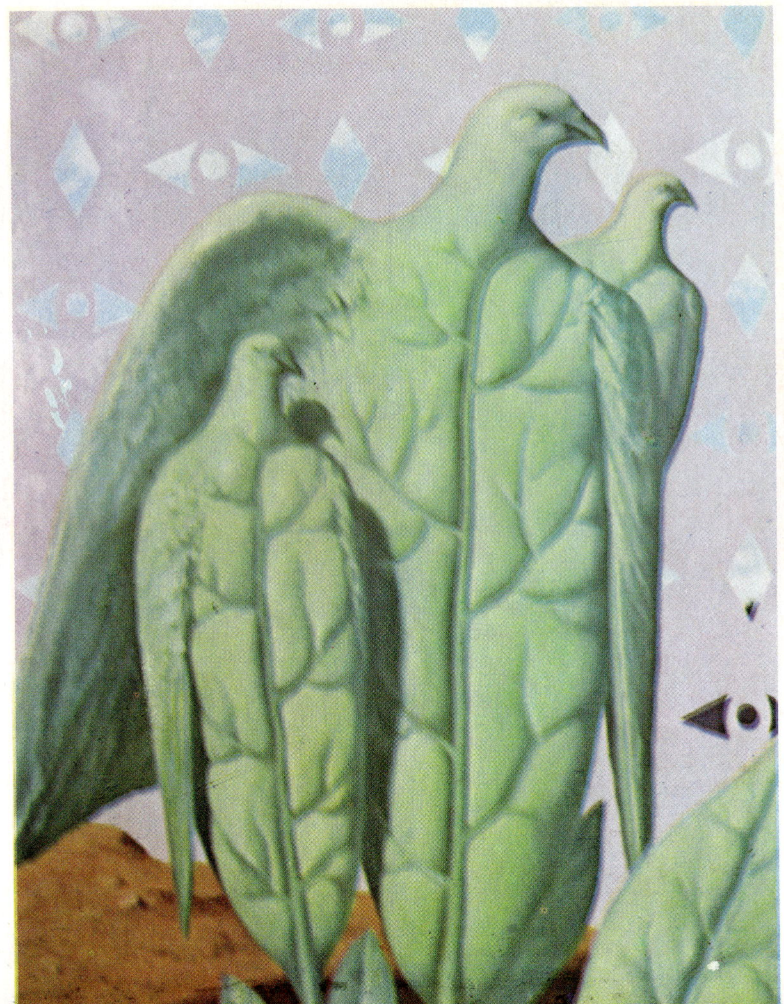

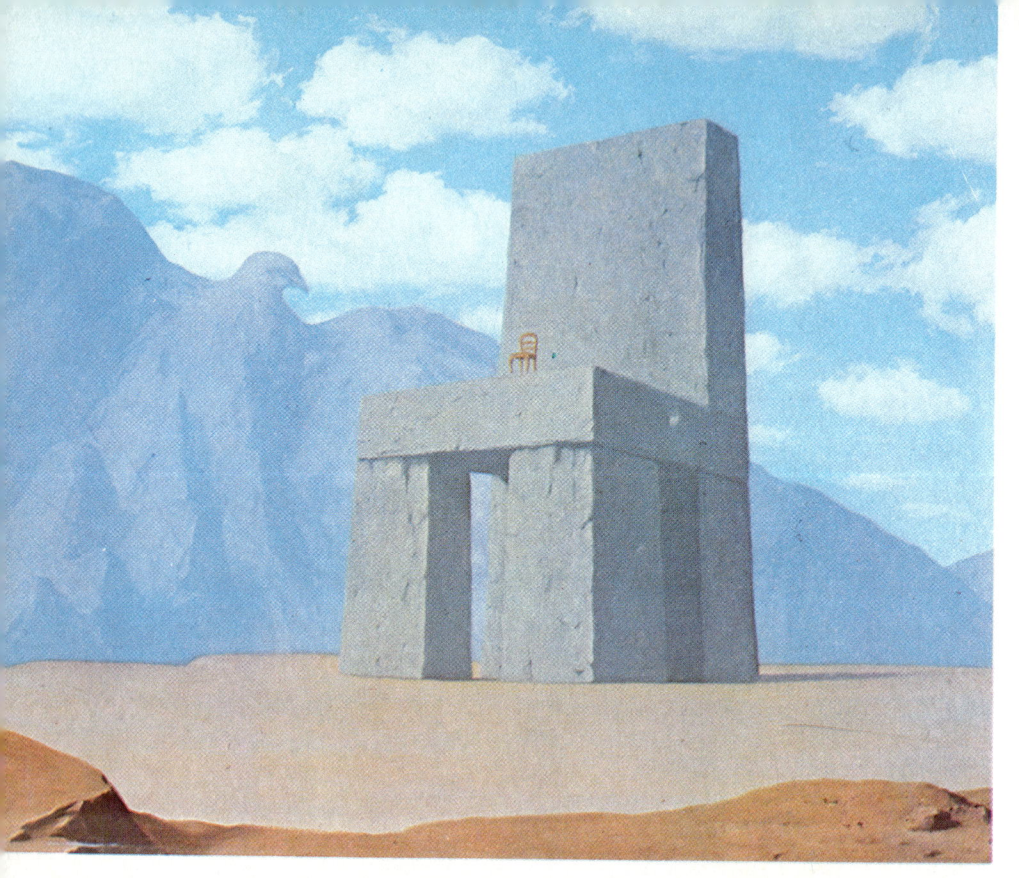

67
The enchanted domain (detail)
1952

68
Arnheim's domain
1962

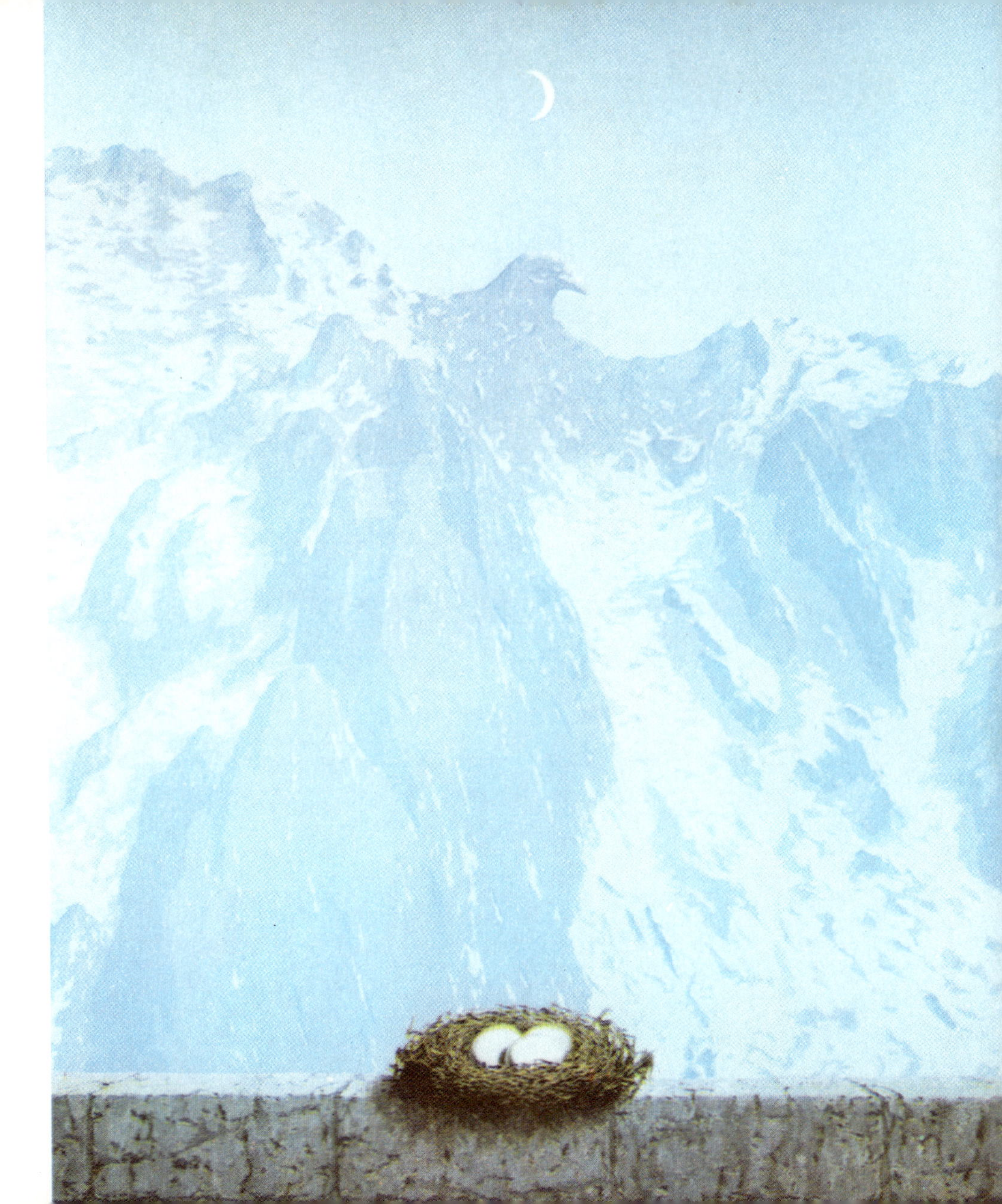

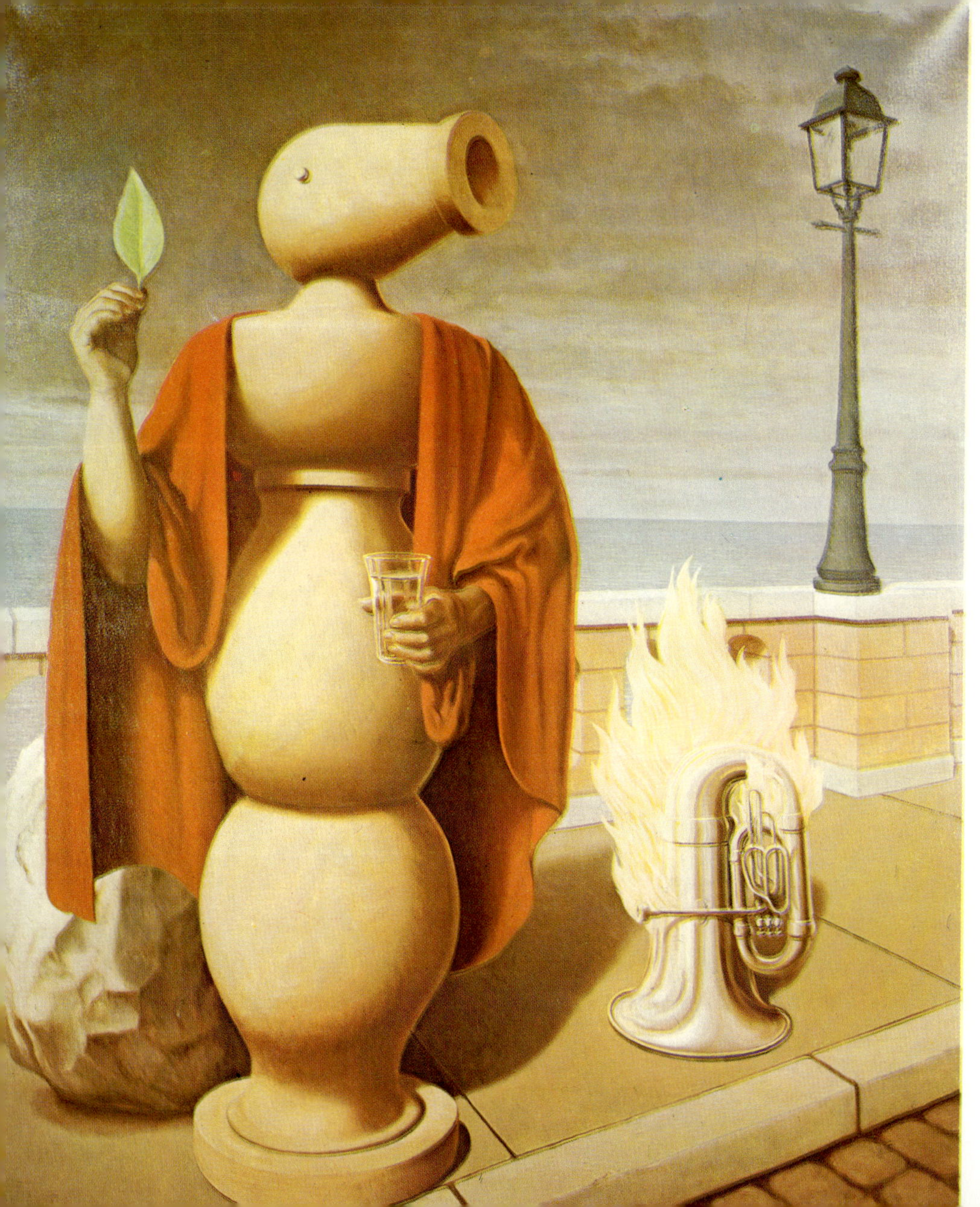

69
The rights of man
1947

70
Untitled

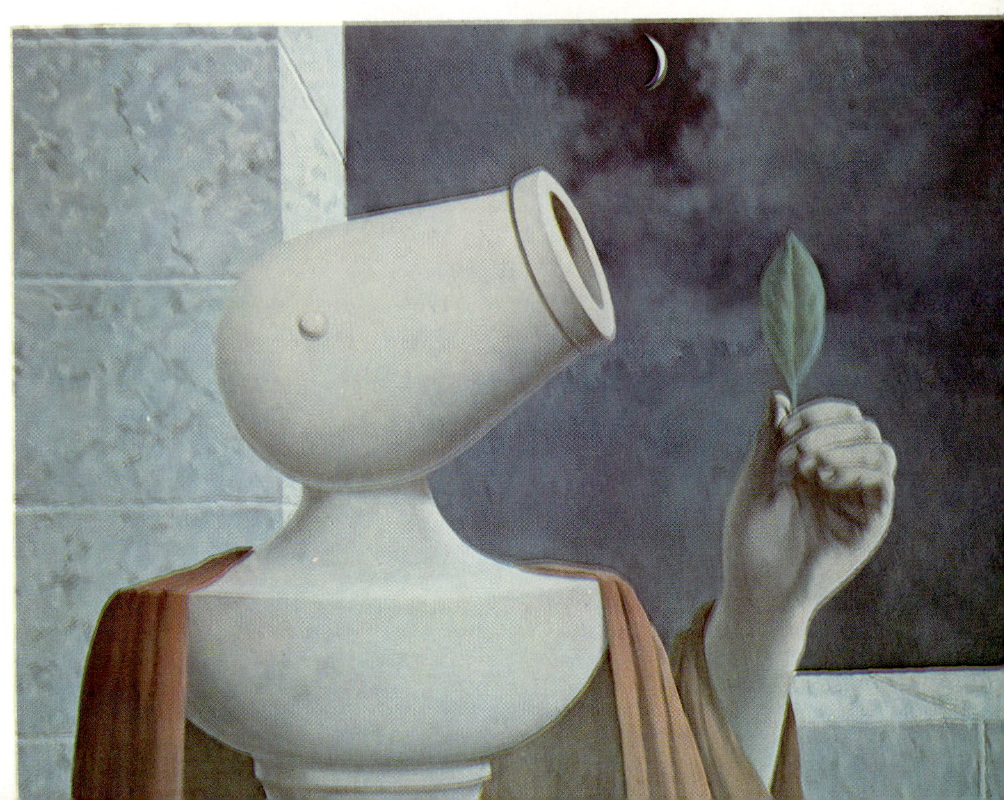

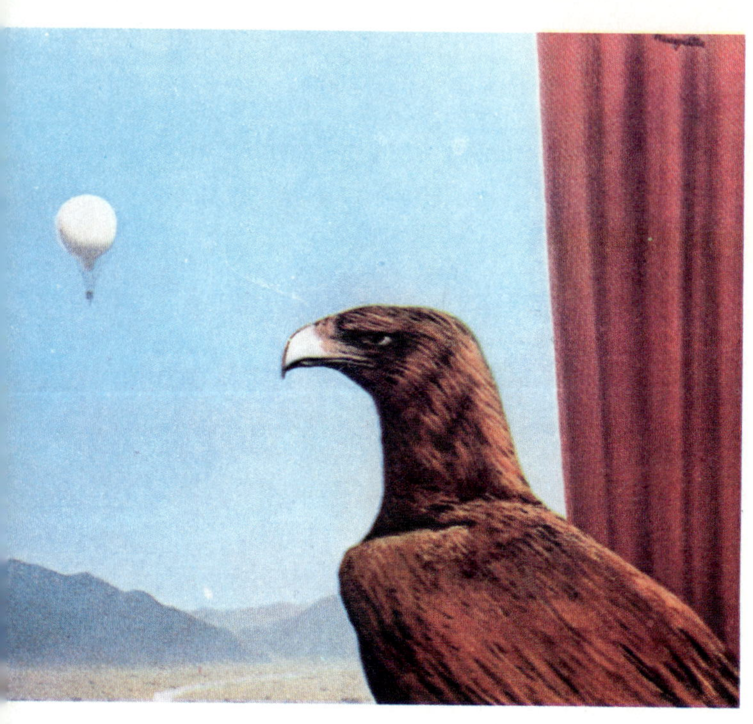

71
The thief
1967

72
When the time is up (detail)
1946

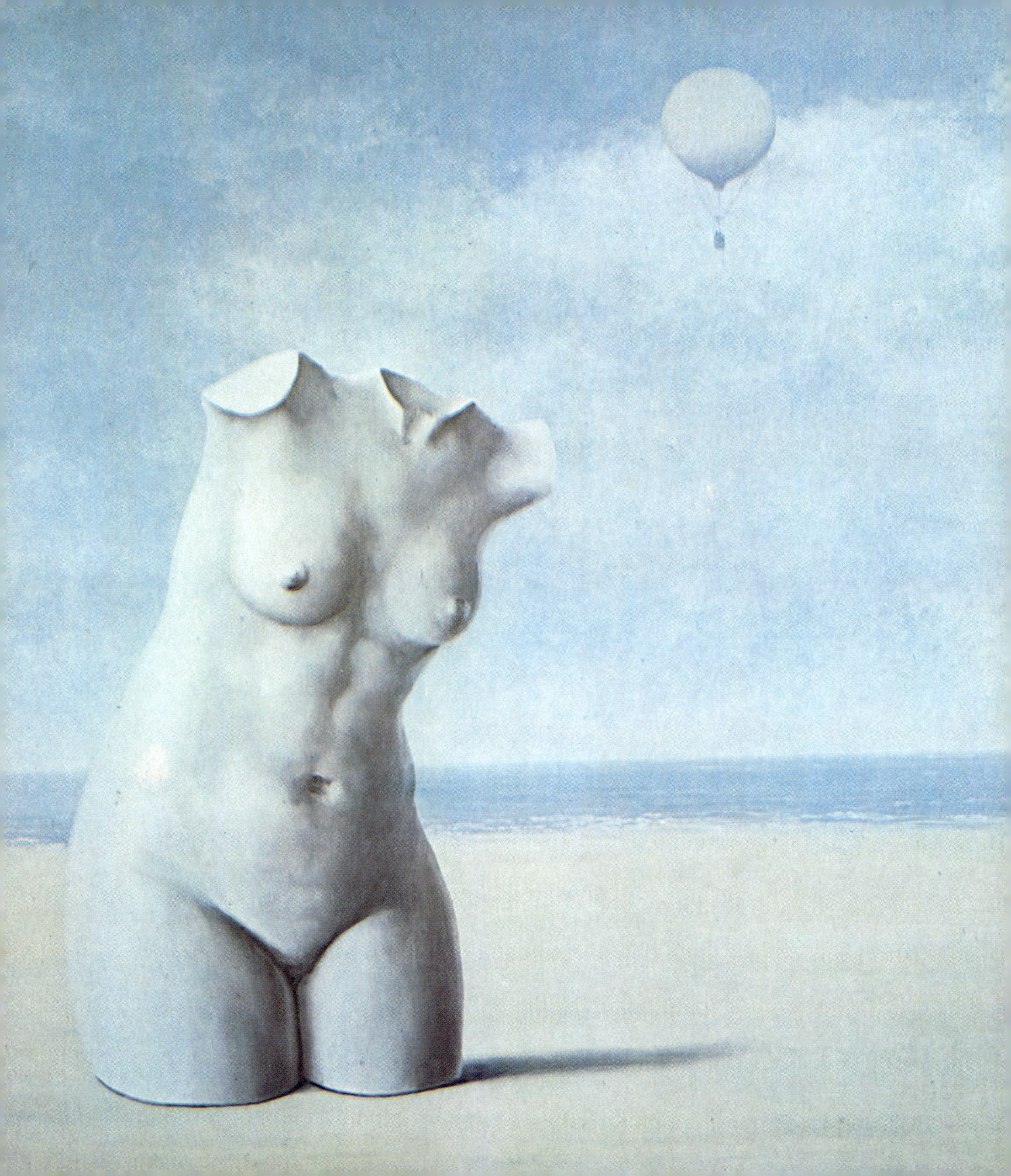

73
The meeting with pleasure
1950

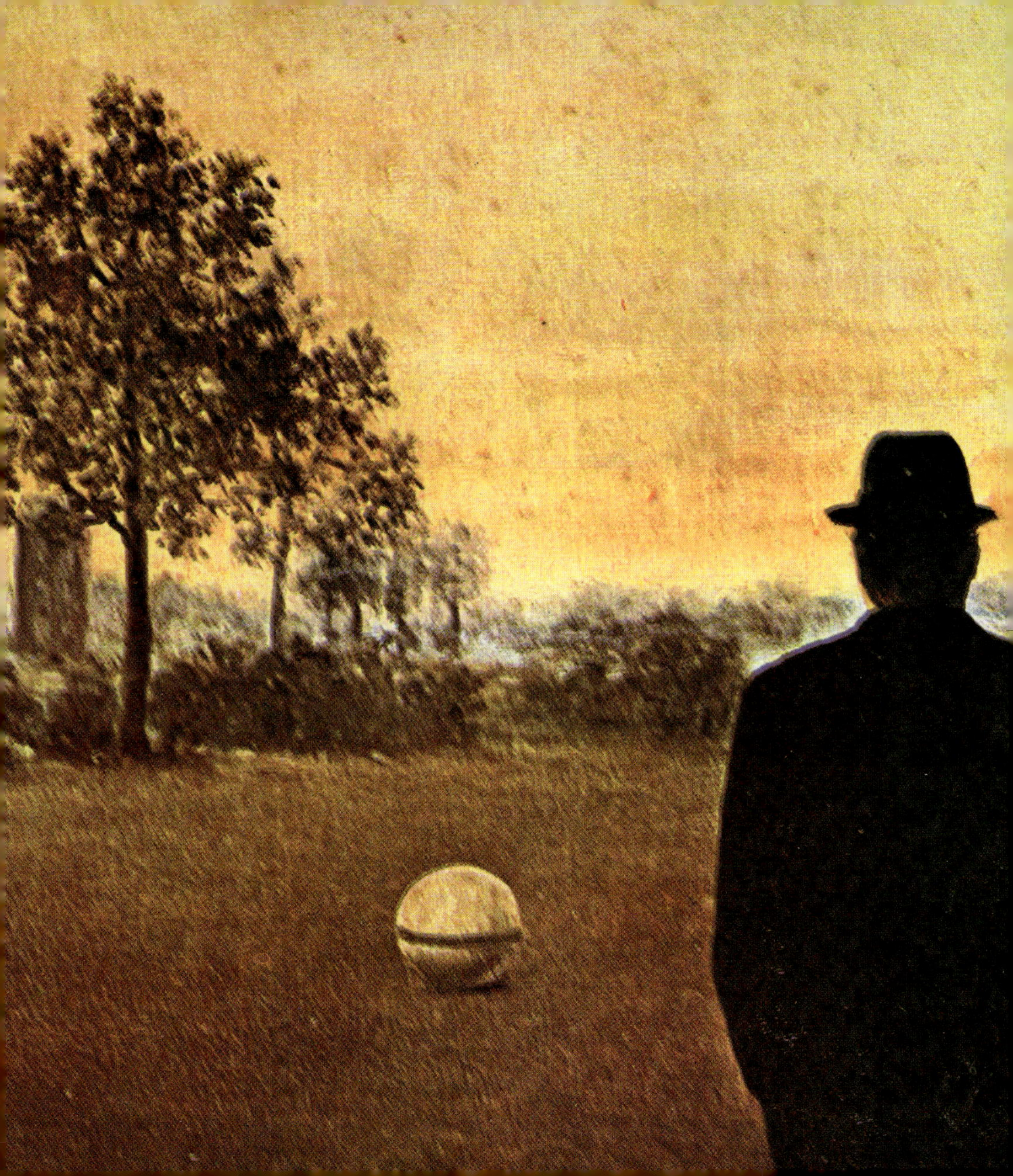

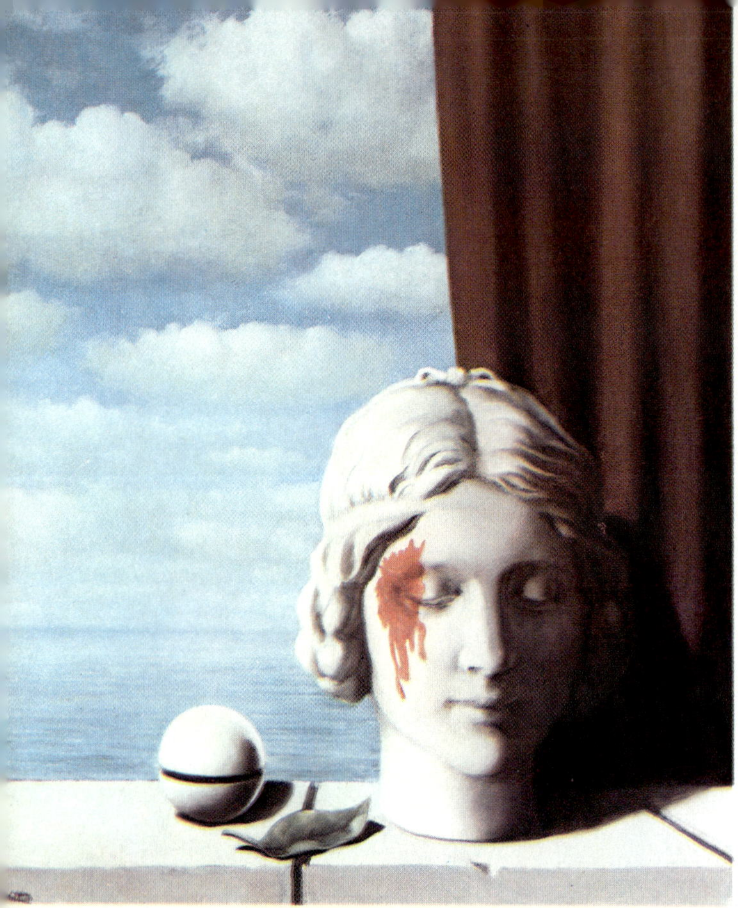

74
Memory
1948

75
Memories of a saint
1961

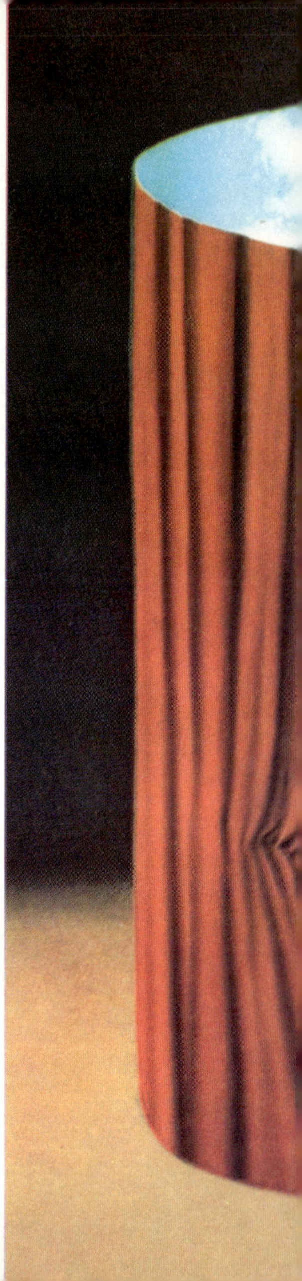

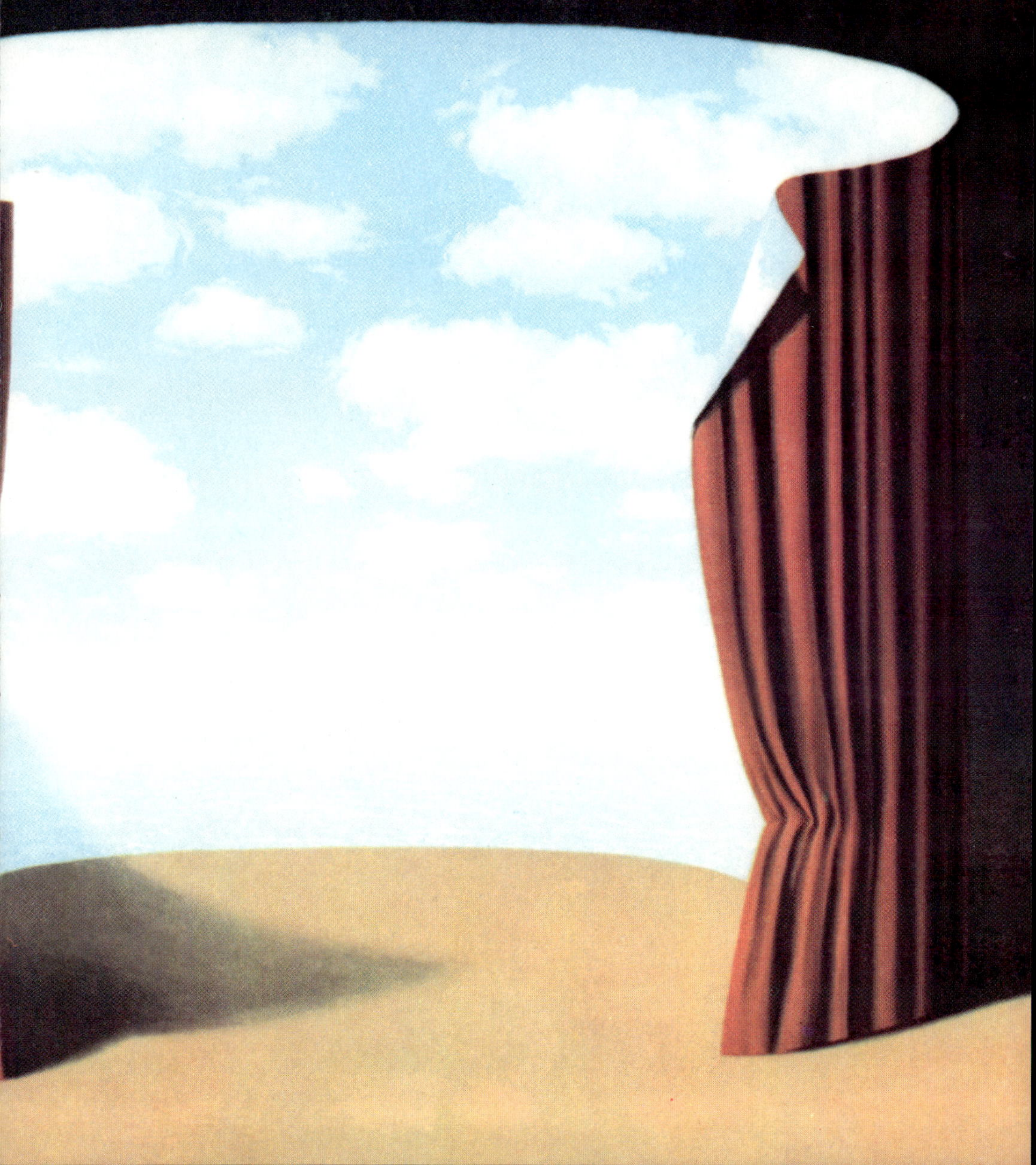

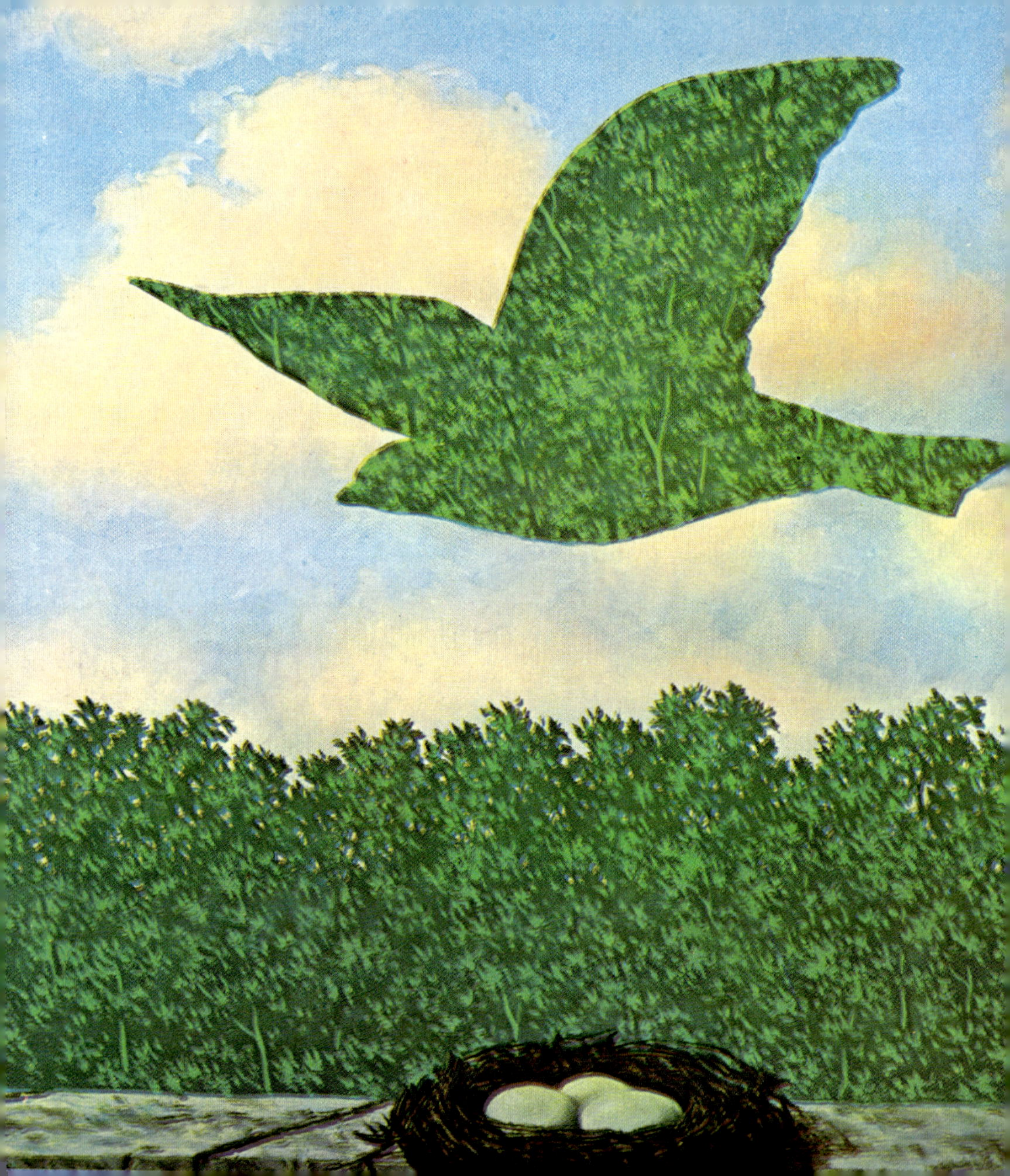

76
Spring (detail)
1965

77
Man with the melon hat
1964

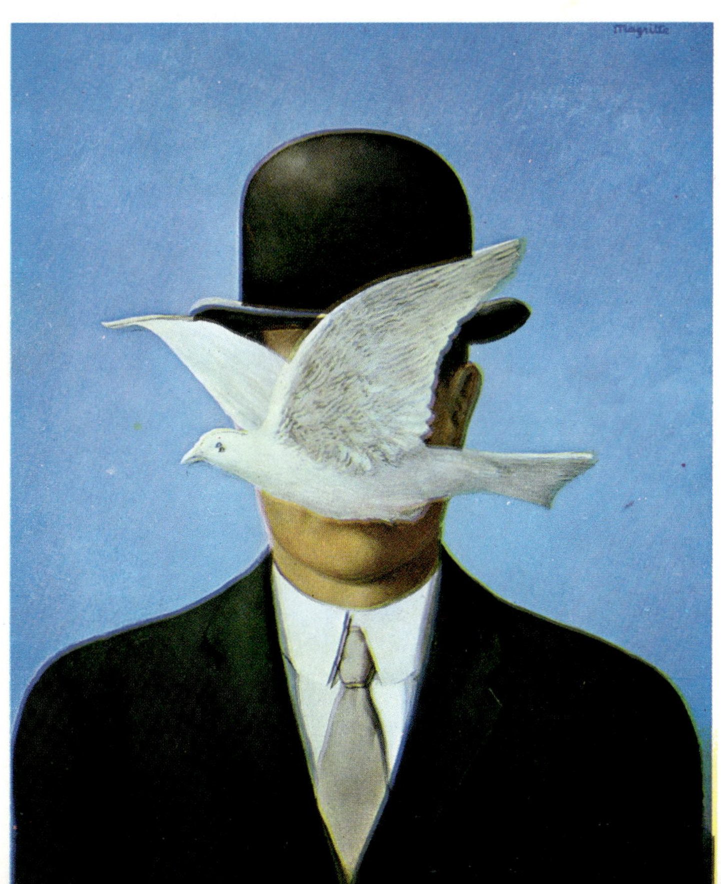

78
The difficult crossing
1967

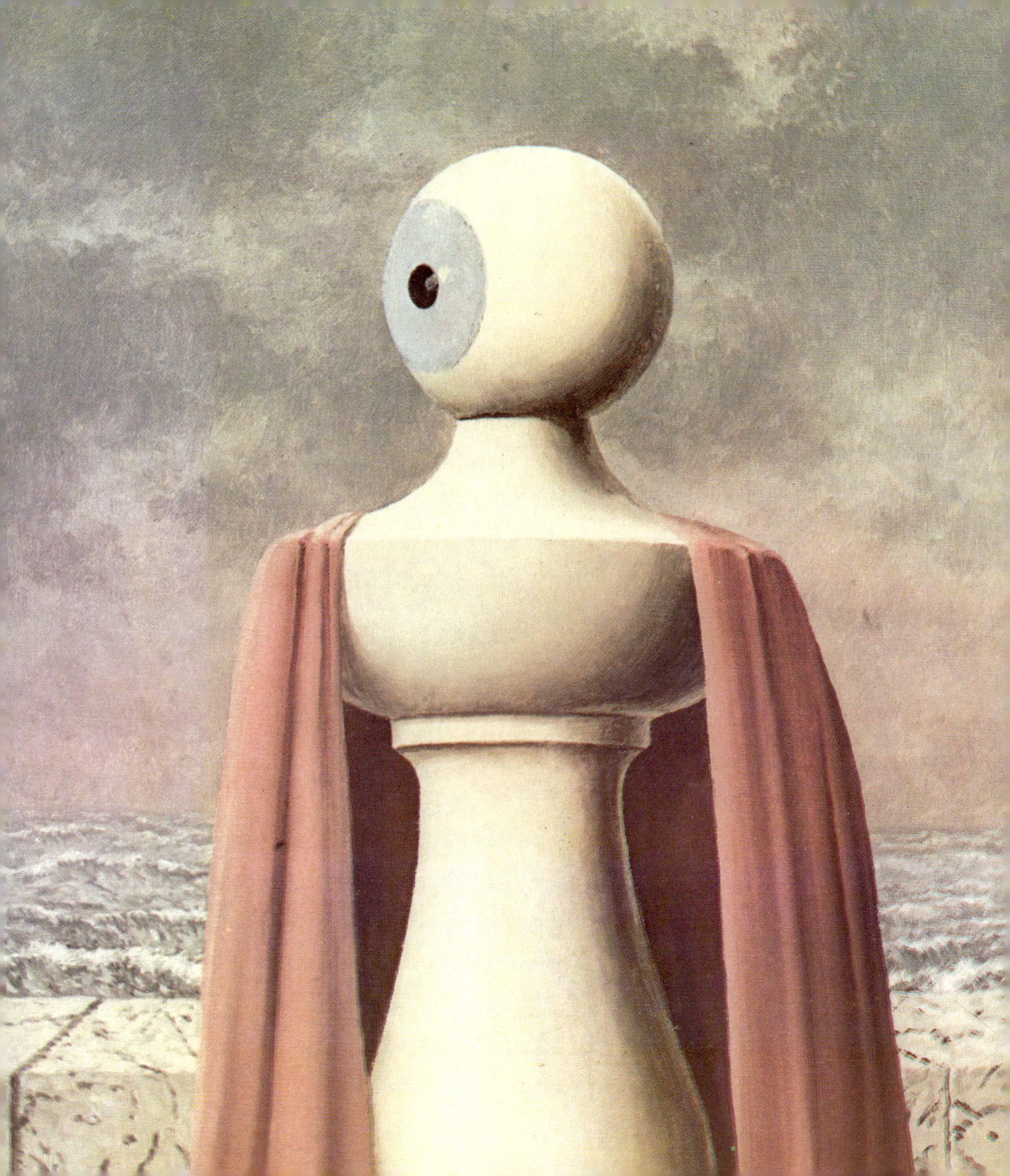

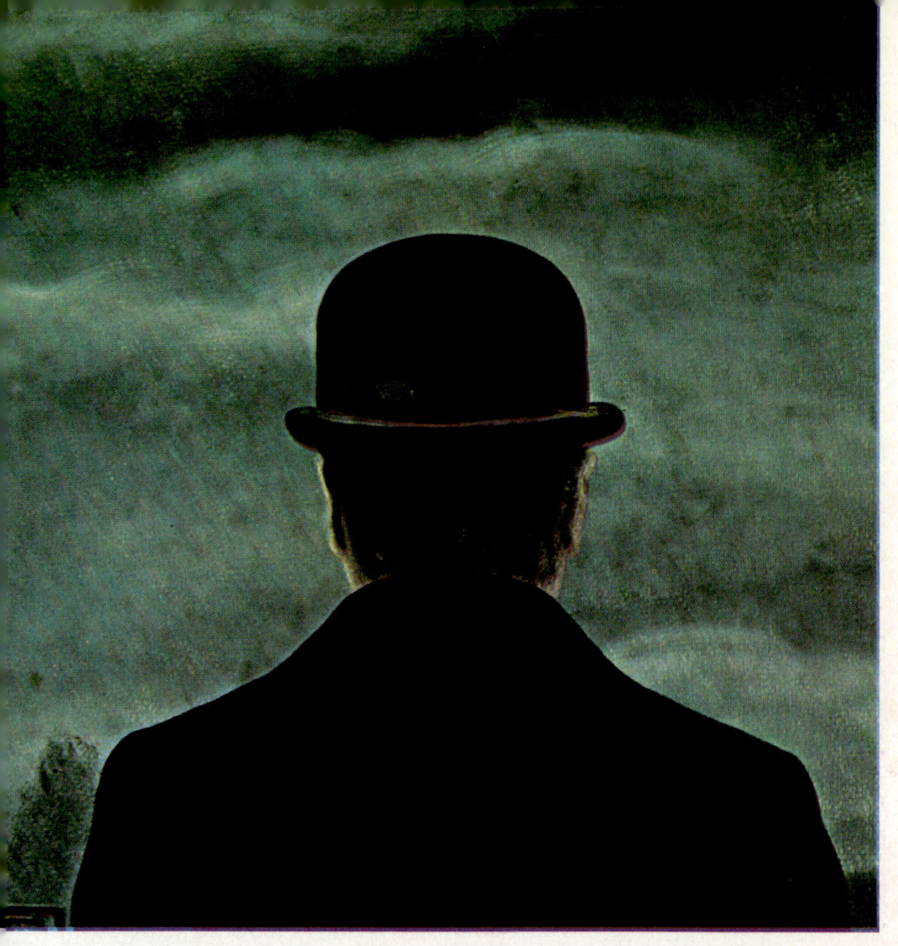

79
Reveries of a solitary walker (detail)
1926